Assertive Confident Communication Skills

A guide to better social skills through assertiveness, effective communication and increased confidence.

Ryan Ledger & Lisa Reynolds

Copyright © Ryan Ledger Publishing

Table of Contents

Effective Communication Can Change Your Life

Being able to communicate effectively is an extremely important skill to have. We communicate with people all day, every day, and our communication skills are vital for being heard and understood by others. Communication allows us to convey information to others, and to understand what messages they are conveying to us.

Communication can take various forms. The most common is verbal communication but it can also be written or even face-to-face non-verbal communication, like gestures and body language.

Humans have an innate need to communicate with others, yet not all of us are naturally gifted at communicating. If you're someone who feels like you're not naturally gifted at communication, you're not alone. Most of us have left a job interview feeling like we didn't get our points across clearly enough. And even more of us have probably left a party where we felt that we stumbled over even the most basic conversations.

Communication skills are especially important in your professional life. Even in roles that don't deal directly with clients or customers, you'll need to at the very least be able to communicate with your boss and your colleagues. For senior roles, advanced communication skills are usually an essential requirement. It's almost impossible to be able to lead and motivate people without the ability to communicate effectively.

In your personal life, your relationships are dependent on you being able to communicate well. Strained relationships between spouses, parents and their children, or even between friends are often directly down to poor communication on one or both sides. When you have the skills to understand the other person's message and respond clearly without misunderstandings, relationships are much more enjoyable and easier to maintain. Communication goes way beyond the words you use and takes into account, not just what you say but how you say it. This is along with the non-verbal signals your body language can convey. It's a vast field of study, and at first glance, the sheer amount of skills required to become a good communicator can seem daunting.

But don't worry! Communication is a skill like any other that can be learned and improved upon one step at a time. Each change you make to the way you communicate will enhance and enrich your relationships, and it will soon become second nature. This book will break down the essential skills for you in a simple and easy to implement way.

So, if you feel like your communication skills aren't as polished as you'd like, this book will cover easy and practical ways to address that.

Real Life Case Study

Louise and Karina both graduated from college with business degrees and a 4.0 GPA. They started their careers at the same multi-national company in the customer service department. After three years, Karina had received three promotions and Louise was still in the same role that she had started in.

Both of them were bright and ambitious, and equally hard-working. Their standard of work was the same. So why did Karina excel, while Louise stayed static?

Karina just had better communication skills.

From the beginning, Karina made sure that her conversations with her line manager were clear and productive. She ensured that her manager understood her ambitions, and she frequently scheduled discussions about her performance.

During these discussions, she was open to feedback and assertively stated her opinions without becoming aggressive or closing down. When dealing with colleagues and managers, she was always aware of her body language and tone of voice and listened carefully to their words before responding.

Louise, however, was incredibly shy and had a tendency to avoid awkward conversations. She also had regular performance reviews with her line manager but would become defensive about feedback points or remain silent with her arms folded.

During meetings with other colleagues, she found that she was nervous about putting her point and opinions across, which led to her not fully listening. Halfway through a colleague's conversation she would be frantically trying to formulate a response in her head – leading her to miss key points that her colleagues had raised. In turn, this left Louise's colleagues feeling frustrated by her lack of listening skills.

As a result, Louise was overlooked for promotions despite being hard working and talented. Karina, on the other hand, was able to stand out due to her advanced communication skills.

Chapter 1 – Communicate More Effectively!

The Amazing Benefits of Good Communication Skills

Louise's experience is all too common but it can be turned around by developing excellent communication skills. We've already mentioned how important good communication skills are in every aspect of our lives but just what kind of benefits can you see from improving your communication skills? Here are a few examples:

Better Relationships
All relationships are built on communication, and good communication is what sustains them over the long term. While someone's appearance might initially attract you to them, it's who they are and how they communicate that to you that makes you want to maintain a relationship.

When your communication skills are lacking, you might find that you are engaged in conflict more than you'd like with people close to you. Perhaps you even feel unheard or underappreciated because you are not communicating well. When you can communicate effectively with the ones you love, relationships become much easier and small misunderstandings can be quickly resolved before they escalate into a bigger problem.

Better Job Satisfaction
In much the same way as personal relationships, good communication is essential at work. When you communicate clearly and effectively at work, you're better able to build good working relationships and to have your opinion heard by your colleagues and superiors.

When you can communicate clearly, meetings and presentations become easier. You can focus on solving the problems at hand instead of getting tangled up in and trying to resolve miscommunications.

You'll find it easier to ask for pay rises, sail through job interviews with ease and be generally more confident at work when you are able to communicate effectively.

Increased Happiness

The side effect of better job satisfaction and better personal relationships is that you will naturally become a happier person. Numerous studies have shown that nurturing strong relationships is one of the biggest keys to happiness that there is – and without communication, we can't have healthy relationships.

Increased Success

Communication skills are essential for success. Whether it's asking for a pay rise, delivering a winning pitch to a potential client or maintaining a happy marriage, communication skills are crucial to your success.

Better Emotional Intelligence

Having great communication skills requires that you are self-aware and aware of others. Being able to communicate well means that you must be able to pick up on people's cues like tone of voice and body language. You also need to be aware of your own – and the impact it has on others.

All of this is also crucial to emotional intelligence – a term coined by Peter Salovey and John D. Mayer and further popularized by Daniel Goleman. It's a term that's well-known among CEOs and leaders and is recognized as an essential leadership skill. However, it's just as important for our personal relationships as it is for professional ones.

Communication is a vital skill for all aspects of modern life, and this book is designed to give you highly practical, easily implementable tips to improve your communication skills. Whether you want to be able to strike up a conversation at parties or get your point across effectively when negotiating a pay increase, this book is for you.

In the following chapters, you will:

- investigate the different types of communication
- learn the importance of listening and reading body language
- identify tools and strategies to confidently communicate in any situation.

Chapter 2 – What's Your Communication Problem?

Commonly Encountered Communication Problems

Not communicating effectively can cause a whole raft of problems in your personal and professional life. If you're not a natural conversationalist, then the chances are that you regularly fall foul of at least one of these problems:

Running Out of Things To Say

Most often, this happens in personal situations when we meet new people at parties or other social gatherings. If you're nervous or feeling awkward, then the conversation can quickly run dry.

If you find that you often rely on the usual generic questions like: So, what do you do? And once the usually brief explanation is done, you find yourself scrabbling around for something else to say. It's a painfully common experience, especially among introverts, but it's easily remedied by developing better small talk skills – something we'll cover in detail later in this book.

Misunderstandings

If you're not a great communicator, then you might find that people sometimes misunderstand the message you are trying to convey, or perhaps even that you misunderstand them. Misunderstandings can be caused by language or cultural barriers, poor word choice, an inappropriate tone of voice or even poor body language.

How people interpret what you say to them depends on a whole host of non-verbal cues. In writing it can be even harder to convey your true meaning if it's anything other than a purely factual statement. Misunderstandings are a great plot device for a fictional story, but in real life, they can leave you feeling embarrassed and anxious. Misunderstandings can often lead to further communication breakdown or unnecessary conflict.

Not Being Taken Seriously

If you struggle to clearly communicate your point of view, you may find yourself overlooked and underestimated at work or indeed at home. You could have the greatest idea in the world, but if you can't put it across to other people in a way they can understand, then you're unlikely to be taken seriously. Not being taken seriously can lead to you feeling frustrated, impact self-esteem and further compound your communication issues. Good communication skills can help you come across more clearly and confidently so that people are more likely to listen to what you have to say.

Conflict

Conflict isn't always a problem, and it can be a necessary and important part of communicating with others. At its root, conflict is simply a variance of interests. If it's handled well, it can allow us to build stronger relationships based on mutual trust and respect.

Unfortunately, many of us find conflict hard to handle because we lack the communication skills necessary to deal with it. When this happens, a normal and healthy disagreement can escalate into an argument and potentially damage relationships and leave us even more nervous about communicating with others. Others may shy away entirely from conflict, thus surrendering the control of the issue or situation to another. As a result, you can be left feeling overwhelmingly frustrated and dissatisfied with the outcome.

Relationship Breakdown

Communication is vital for all your personal relationships. In romantic relationships, it's especially important. In fact, a breakdown in communication is cited in a staggering number of divorces.

It's important to be able to express yourself to your nearest and dearest in a way that enhances your relationships. Unfortunately, we don't always communicate well with each other for numerous reasons. We might be so afraid of rejection that we don't communicate our true feelings, or so afraid of conflict that we don't air grievances. On the flip side of that, we might air our grievances a little too often, or in an aggressive way that makes our partner feel personally attacked.

Communication is just as important for friendships and your relationships with your own children or other family members as it is in a romantic relationship. Often, we expect the people closest to us to simply understand us as if by magic, but without good communication, they can't be expected to pick up on our wants and needs.

Possible Causes for Communication Problems

The *'symptoms'* of poor communication just listed are often linked to a handful of root causes. By identifying what is the root cause of your communication issue, you'll be more easily able to rectify it.

Social Anxiety and Shyness

Social anxiety is very common, and while it's something

we often link with introverts, you may be surprised to learn that it can affect extroverts just as much. Social anxiety often leads to people finding small talk difficult and in addition to this, being assertive enough to get their point across. It can lead to you shying away from important conversations, leaving you feeling frustrated and 'unheard.' You may have developed your social anxiety as a young child, or perhaps a significant life event or unpleasant experience as an adult knocked your confidence and caused the anxiety.

You can often help reduce shyness and anxiety by educating yourself about them and putting into practice the skills to overcome them. If your issues are fairly mild, then simply applying the techniques in this book should help, but in the first instance, you should always seek advice from a trained professional. In more extreme cases, a trained therapist may be required to help you overcome any social anxiety that you are feeling.

Low Self-Esteem
People with low self-esteem can find it very hard to be assertive and will often 'clam up' when faced with someone louder or more insistent. If you have low self-esteem, it can be difficult to assert yourself, and your posture or body language might make you appear an 'easy target' or uncommunicative if left unchecked.

Low self-esteem can make you feel like you aren't as intelligent, sociable, or witty as other people. It can make starting or joining conversations seem terrifying. You may constantly be experiencing negative thoughts, wondering if other people can pick up on your perceived flaws.

If you suffer from low self-esteem, there are ways to improve this, and we'll look at these more closely in

Chapter 8.

Communication Barriers

Communication barriers are things like cultural differences, language barriers, or even the environment itself. Even somebody's emotional state can be a barrier to communication. For example, people will react differently to criticism when they are under great personal stress, compared to when they are happy. Of course, not all communication barriers can be removed, and some of them – such as emotional barriers can be hard to spot. Luckily, there are still plenty of ways to reduce their effect and make sure that you are communicating as clearly as possible, regardless of barriers.

We'll look more closely at communication barriers and how to overcome them a little later in this book.

Being Too Passive

Particularly if you feel like you're not taken seriously, the issue could be that you are too passive. If you back down very quickly and seek to avoid conflict at all costs, people may begin to see you as a *'pushover.'* So, when your needs don't match with theirs, they will simply assume that you will back down. Passive people often fail to stand up for themselves and express their feelings, needs, or opinions. They also tend to make little or no eye contact and speak in a soft tone of voice or use apologetic language.

This can be an issue not only in the workplace but also in romantic relationships and parenting struggles. The other downside of being passive is that you can begin to feel resentful that you're unable to be heard and can even start to feel hopeless or depressed.

Being Too Aggressive

Assertion and aggression are very different and being aggressive in communications is rarely a productive choice. At best, the other person will simply disengage from the conversation, and at worst it could turn into an argument or physically threatening altercation that damages the relationship.

It's a common assumption that being aggressive will get you what you want – especially if the other person isn't particularly aggressive but in reality, it's just a form of bullying. Communicating in an aggressive manner is more likely to make the other person respond in the same way, become passive-aggressive or simply walk away entirely from the conversation.

In contrast, assertive communicators are clear and firm but don't force the other person to adopt an aggressive or defensive stance. We'll explore the differences between aggression and assertion later in the book.

Sarcasm and Passive-Aggressiveness
Passive-aggression or sarcasm may seem harmless enough, but if it's a common feature in your communications, you may come across as condescending and even plain old nasty. In important conversations, it can get in the way of finding a positive solution and can put other people on the defensive very quickly.

People who tend to be sarcastic will often defend their sarcasm, claiming it to be *'just a joke.'* But sarcasm is generally just hostility dressed up as humor. In fact, the word sarcasm originates from the Greek word *"sarkazein"* – meaning *"to tear or strip the flesh off."*

In small doses, or in the right company, a little sarcasm might be welcome but if in doubt it's always better to avoid it altogether.

Over-Emotional or Blaming Language

If you're trying to get your point across, few things will turn off the listener faster than if you seem to be blaming them or are overly emotional. Of course, there are always situations that are emotional in nature, but make sure it's an appropriate setting. Letting your emotions out in a heart-to-heart with a close friend is perfectly natural, normal and healthy. Yet allowing too much emotion to seep into regular conversations or professional exchanges can cause communications to go downhill fast.

Of course, not all emotions are negative, and there are appropriate times and places to embrace emotive communication. However, if you're angry, frustrated or upset, then it's usually best to avoid allowing that to seep into your communications. It rarely helps and often hinders, productive communication.

Not Listening

All too often we hear what someone else is saying, but we don't really listen. Not listening effectively can lead to miscommunications, misunderstandings, and conflict. Sometimes you may think you're listening, when in fact you're not. Not listening to someone can be subtler than the obvious situations where your mind wanders to unrelated things while a person is speaking.

If you find yourself thinking of your response while the other person is still speaking, or you speak before they are finished, these are signs of not listening effectively.

Personality Clashes

We've all heard the adage *'speak to others as you would wish to be spoken to.'* On the surface, it seems like sound advice, and in respect of treating others with courtesy and respect, it works.

However, we all have different personalities, and taking this advice to the extreme could have a detrimental impact on your communications. For example, one person may be a mild-mannered and polite person, who uses a lot of *'softening'* language. They may take time to build up to making a point, especially if they feel it may not be well-received by the other person.

In contrast, the person they are speaking to may be a very direct person, who tends to keep all emotion out of conversations and prefers to get right to the point.

Neither personality type or communication style is wrong – they simply have different preferences. However, the direct person may come across as rude to the polite person, while the polite person may come across as bumbling to the direct person. One of the most useful communication skills is having the ability to speak to others as they would wish to be spoken to.

But how do you know what someone else's preferences are, and how exactly do you adapt to that without compromising your own communication style?

In the next chapter, we'll look at the different communication styles and how to identify your own communication style. We'll also investigate how to spot what style someone else is using, and how you can adapt to their style to improve communication.

Chapter 3 – What's Your Communication Type?

"To effectively communicate, we must realize that we are all different in the way we perceive the world and use this understanding as a guide to our communication with others."
Tony Robbins

Identifying Communication Types

There are four basic common communication types: *Passive, Aggressive, Passive-Aggressive* and *Assertive.*

Having a good understanding of these four basic styles of communication can help you understand how you are communicating, and how that might come across to others. It will also help you recognize when you may be able to change the way you communicate in order to better connect with the person you are speaking with.

Your default communication style may be unconscious, but it's amazing how once you have the right level of awareness, you can choose how to communicate. It can almost instantly improve your communication skills when you're self-aware about your own communication style. It can be easy to blame other people for not understanding us, but the first rule of effective communication is: The success of the communication is the responsibility of the communicator.

So, let's look at these four basic styles in more depth:

Passive

People who use a passive communication style tend to be quiet, and submissive in their communications. If they venture an opinion or idea at all, they will quickly yield to an opposing opinion. Passive communicators are rarely able to openly express their feelings or needs, which can lead to frustration or resentment. They also rarely say no, in an attempt to avoid confrontation or conflict, and so they are easily taken advantage of. The body language of a passive communicator tends to be very closed. They rarely hold eye contact and may sit or stand in a slumped position.

One of the positives of passive communicators is that they can be seen as good listeners. While that's not always necessarily true, a passive communicator is unlikely to steamroller you with their own opinion. So, when someone is feeling fragile and needs to vent, they may seek out a passive communicator to talk to. Passive communicators also have a tendency to *'go with the flow'* and not disrupt anything, and so they're often easy to get along with.

The kind of phrases you may hear from a passive communicator are:

- *"I don't mind..."*
- *"I must have misunderstood..."*
- *"I'm sure I'll be able to find the time to do that for you.."*

Aggressive
Aggressive communicators are easy to identify, by their usually loud and domineering manner. They may speak in a loud voice, hold eye contact for longer than necessary, or use gestures like pointing while speaking.
Aggressive communicators tend to try to dominate others and control the conversation or outcome by using strong-handed tactics like threats, blame, and intimidation. At

their worst, they are rude and domineering, but their aggressive style gets them heard and can sometimes lead to them becoming viewed as a leader.

The kind of phrases you may hear from an aggressive communicator are:

- *"Mark my words…"*
- *"I told you not to…"*
- *"This is your fault…"*
- *"This is not open for discussion…"*

Passive-Aggressive

Passive-aggressive communicators may appear to be passive at first, but on closer investigation, there's a difference. At the core of passive-aggressive communication is a feeling of resentment that the individual feels unable to directly express. Unlike the aggressive communicator, who will openly confront someone, the passive-aggressive communicator will tend to seethe in silence and react in very subtle, but still potentially relationship damaging ways.

They may become overly pleasant, to the point of it being comical, or their facial expressions may seem at odds with their tone of voice and word choice. They may appear co-operative on the surface while actually being obstructive. For example, they might agree to complete an action and then purposefully ignore it, claiming later that they forgot or providing some other excuse if challenged.

For passive-aggressive communicators, body language is often a key indicator. They're also more likely than other types to give someone the silent treatment or to spread malicious rumors.

The kind of phrases you may hear from a passive-aggressive communicator are:

- *"If you really want to..."*
- *"I hope you don't mind, but..."*
- *"Correct me if I'm wrong..."*

Assertive
Generally considered the most effective form of communication, an assertive communication style combines the best parts of the other communication styles.

Assertive communicators can confidently express their own needs, desires, ideas, and feelings just like the aggressive communicator. However, the difference is that assertive communicators do this calmly while also taking the needs of others into account. They can see the other person's side of things just like the passive communicator and are able to concede when they feel it's the right thing to do.

Assertive communicators tend to balance their own needs with the needs of others and look for a solution that meets as many people's needs as possible. They do this without conceding on anything that's very important to them. Like aggressive communicators, assertive people don't shy away from confrontation. However, unlike aggressive communicators, assertive people don't invite it, and their style actually tends to deflect and diffuse conflict. Sometimes the differences in word choice between an aggressive communicator and an assertive communicator can seem subtle – but the effect on communication is astounding.

For example, an aggressive communicator may say *"You upset me when you said..."* whereas an assertive communicator may *say "I felt upset when you said...".* By changing the emphasis to *"I",* they are removing some of the blame, taking ownership of feelings and giving the other person space to consider what they say without immediately becoming defensive.

The kind of phrases you may hear from an assertive communicator are:

- *"Thanks for the invitation, but I already have plans that evening."*
- *"I get frustrated when you don't appear to be listening to me."*

These four types are useful but are just a simplistic overview of communication styles. There are other models of communication styles, and these can differ depending on the context of the communication.

Communicating in Personal Relationships

Personal relationships are any relationships we have with friends and family. Of course, the most intense type of personal relationship is between romantic partners and so we'll focus on this here. However, the information and the types we will discuss here can be equally applied to all kinds of interpersonal relationships. You can apply the same communication styles to friendships, although the differences are often less amplified.

Few situations amplify our communication differences more than a romantic relationship. Most of us have experienced the frustration that having different communication styles can bring.
Perhaps you like to resolve issues immediately, and your

partner needs a lot of time to think things through. Or perhaps you feel that your partner doesn't appreciate you because they rarely express their feelings to you, yet they seem baffled that this upsets you.

All too often, what seem like small differences and quirks early in a relationship can widen to a chasm between you over time. Luckily, most of these differences can be resolved by simply improving your own communication skills.

You don't have to get to a place where you both communicate in the exact same way – it was your own unique personalities that brought you together, after all! In fact, viewing one way as the only right way is a sure fire way to compound any communication problems you have.

It's more about understanding and respecting each other's personal communication styles, and making small compromises to ensure you each feel heard and understood. Your partner's communication style might drive you crazy at first, but it's not necessarily a better or worse way than your own – simply different. Our styles are affected by multiple factors. Age, gender, culture, previous relationships, how our parents communicated… the list is endless. And we're often not even aware of how our communication style is affected by all of these background filters.

By learning more about your own and your partner or future partner's communication style, and taking steps to understand it, you can bridge any gaps that you come across.

Reducers and Expanders
A reducer tends to offer as little information as possible.

They will provide the minimum they think you need to understand their point. They find too much detail distracting and will attempt to *'get to the point'* in the most efficient manner possible. Often, some of the *'detail'* that reducers consider distractions are feelings and emotions. They often sound quite unemotive – which is useful in some situations but can be frustrating for their romantic partners who are trying to understand how they feel.

On the other hand, the expanders will provide all of the detail and description they possibly can. They frequently talk about feelings and emotions, and they tend to enjoy sharing conversation rather than seeing it as a means to communicate a specific point. Reducers and expanders can find each other confusing at best and frustrating at worst. Reducers find all the detail and description provided by expanders to be distracting. They may even feel overwhelmed by the level of detail shared.

Expanders can be frustrated at the lack of detail that reducers provide. They may also feel a lack of intimacy because of the reducers tendency to not verbalize their thoughts and feelings as openly as they do.

You're most likely a reducer if:

- *You get frustrated when people include details that aren't directly relevant to the story.*
- *You tend to speak in short sentences.*
- *You're more concerned with practical matters than with emotional ones.*

You're most likely an expander if:

- *You like to hear about all the little details.*
- *You like to share how you feel.*

- *When you tell a story you include details such as what people were wearing.*

Competitive and Collaborative

Competitive communicators seek power and lean towards a more dominant communication style than affiliative communicators. They can be quite direct and challenging, and they will make decisions without feeling the need to consult others.

Collaborative communicators want to work out problems by working together. When a decision needs to be made, they consult others during the decision-making process and consider their opinion before deciding on a course of action.

Collaborators often find being challenged directly, too aggressive.

You're may be competitive if:

- *You make decisions for you both without consulting your partner.*
- *You like to 'win' in an argument.*
- *You will challenge others in order to get your own way.*

You're maybe collaborative if:

- *You tend to check with your partner before making plans.*
- *You like to discuss the pros and cons of an action before you do it.*
- *You don't feel that you must win every argument.*
- *You're happier when everyone is happy, rather than when you're 'right'.*

Direct and Indirect

Most of us fall into one of these two camps when addressing issues or discussing what we need from another person. A direct person tends to get straight to the point. If their partner hasn't washed the dishes and they're not happy about it – they simply come out and say it.

An indirect person won't address the issue directly, and will instead make hints, or *'talk around'* the issue. By doing this, they are expecting the other partner to pick up on what they need from them. While direct is often better for avoiding misunderstandings, it can cause hurt feelings. Indirect communicators are unlikely to offend anyone, but they are more likely to be misunderstood. They run the risk of the other person not picking up correctly on their needs and wants.

Direct communicators can help soften the impact of their directness by thinking through their word choice before speaking and making sure that they are *'softening'* the blow where necessary. Indirect communicators can help their more direct partners understand their needs better by making sure that they are more specific and direct about issues that are important to them.

Both types would benefit from applying the principles of assertive communication to their own styles.

You're probably direct if:

- *You say what's on your mind with little or no thought about how to position it.*
- *You take pride in getting to the point.*

You're probably indirect if:

- *You think carefully about how to say something*

- *You'd rather avoid confrontation or hurting someone's feelings*

Communication In The Workplace

Communication styles for the workplace have a lot of similarities with the personal relationship communication styles. However, the way you communicate at home and at work can be very different, and some slightly different approaches are required in a workplace or any formal setting.

Dynamic
Dynamic communicators are very charismatic. They tend to be animated when they speak, using facial expressions and gestures to complement their words. They are confident when they speak, and they make decisions quickly and confidently too.

Dynamic communicators are often good with words and use strong, impactful words when speaking to others. They can be quite persuasive and know how to hold an audience. They are comfortable speaking in public or doing the rounds at networking events and conferences.

Logical
Logical communicators are very practical and like to rely on facts and data when presenting an argument. They place a high value on evidence and dislike spurious claims without facts to back them up.

They are very practical and don't tend to use emotive language to make their points. They tend to have strong opinions, which they can usually back up with evidence. They often get straight to the point with little or no preamble.

Connected
Connected communicators are very people-focused and good listeners. They may not be the most charismatic person in the room, but they are often the friendliest. They tend to be very approachable and are also empathetic. They take an intuitive approach and prefer to follow their gut feelings rather than rely purely on evidence. This tendency can make them appear to have very subjective opinions.

Connected communicators are considerate of others and encourage discussion among people to come to a solution or conclusion rather than making an outright decision themselves.

You may recognize your own style or other people's style in these descriptions. This isn't an exhaustive list. It's possible to switch between any and all of these styles unconsciously depending on who you're talking to and the context of the conversation. Part of building great communication skills is building an awareness of your preferred styles, and how to consciously adapt to better complement the person or people you are speaking to.

Communication and Personality Types

Personality types can also influence communication styles. There are numerous personality type models available including Myers Briggs and Enneagram types. However, a very simple model that fits well with the four basic styles of communication model is the colors model.

This model basically separates people into red, blue, yellow and green depending on how logical, emotional, introverted and outgoing they are. The analysis can get very detailed, but for the purposes of this book, we'll be keeping it simple. The goal isn't to have in-depth knowledge of personality types – you just need to be able to spot key signs to adapt your own communication style.

Understanding these basic personality types can help you to understand not only how someone is communicating, but also what might be driving that.

Red
Red personality types are competitive, confident and extroverted. They love to win, and they thrive on a challenge. They can sometimes be selfish and domineering, and they become uneasy if they can't exert control over a situation. They often have a 'my way or the highway' attitude and can be very impatient and demanding of others.

They are swift and decisive decision makers, and they are good at getting fast results. For this reason, red personalities can often be found in leadership roles, heading up committees and anywhere that they can be in the spotlight and take charge. Red personalities are also great at solving problems, and their tenacity means that they will stick with a challenge through to the end. They excel at multi-tasking and love to stay busy.

As a communicator, reds are usually direct, competitive and dynamic. They are very capable of adopting an assertive style of communication, but under stress, they may adopt an aggressive communication style.

At the heart of what drives them is a need to achieve and to be recognized.

Blue

Blue personality types are introverted and tend to be very analytical. They pay attention to detail and can be prone to worrying too much from overanalyzing. They are often quiet and avoid social gatherings, but can be quite charming when they are in a sociable mood.

They are usually unemotional, preferring the reliability of hard facts and data to emotions. They dislike dealing with people who are very emotive in conversations. They like to be right and feel threatened if they are challenged harshly. They can have a tendency towards perfectionism.

Their precise nature makes them very thorough, and also very diplomatic. Because they leave emotions out of their dealings with other people they are often a very calming influence. As a communicator, blues are usually direct, reducers, and logical. They can tend to lean towards passive and passive-aggressive communication styles if they feel threatened or uncomfortable.

Green

Greens are people-focused introverts. Being liked is important to them, and they place a high value on feelings and emotions. They do their best to keep the peace in most situations and are very empathetic and supportive of others. Sometimes greens can become people-pleasers, who put the needs of others before their own. They value safety, security and emotional connection and may become easily offended by more direct personalities like reds.

Greens tend to dislike change and can be quite indecisive at times, relying on others to take the lead. They can also be very lenient with others, as they tend to see the positives in people.

As a communicator, greens are usually collaborative, expanders, and connected. Their desire to keep the peace can make them adopt a passive communication style, and they rarely become aggressive.

Yellow

Yellow personality types are the life and soul of the party. They are extroverts, like reds, but they are much less serious and competitive. They often seem impervious to stress and can laugh off most situations that others would find stressful. They are optimistic, friendly and enthusiastic. They do enjoy a challenge and being the center of attention but they don't feel the same need as reds to win. Yellows are very loyal and they enjoy spending time with others. They tend to have a large circle of friends and are often creative, arty types.

They can be very vocal and loud, but they dislike conflict and prefer to keep people happy. They will attempt to keep the peace if conflict seems likely, but they are confident enough to handle conflict if it does actually arise. They can have a tendency to be overconfident and impulsive, and their need for constant socializing can be draining to the introverted green and blue types.

As a communicator, yellows are usually collaborative, expanders, and dynamic. They are often quite assertive but can fall into passive behaviors when trying to maintain peace.

As you can see, there are numerous personality types and communication styles, and various models designed to try and explain them. Luckily, we don't need to get too bogged down into the psychology of it all in order to improve our own communication. Just having an awareness of how you tend to communicate, and what drives it is enough to allow you to change your style to benefit you.

It's important to note that no style is more valid than another, and you can't change someone else's communication style. However, by acknowledging that another person has a style different to your own, you can see more clearly that they may not be trying to frustrate, annoy or upset you. They simply approach communication differently to you.

This awareness can not only help you to get along with others but also help you to understand how others might perceive your own communication style during a conversation.

While all the styles are valid, in the majority of cases, adopting an assertive style of communication is preferable. Most readers of this book will find that their natural style is not an assertive style – as assertive communicators would rarely feel that they needed additional help communicating well. We'll take a look in the next chapter at exactly why assertive communication style is the best style to adopt in almost every situation.

Chapter 4 – Exploring The Effectiveness Of Each Communication Style

"There is a fine line between assertiveness and being relaxed."
Justin Guarini

Communication Style Compatibility in Various Situations

It's true that there are situations where something other than an assertive style will work best. Not every single situation is a time for assertiveness. It's the most effective style in the majority of situations, but if it feels wrong, don't push it.

For example, if you find yourself facing someone you know to be violent, it may not be safe for you to be assertive. Or perhaps you know that a friend is having a bad day and they are needing a rant. You don't have to address everything you don't agree with for the sake of simply asserting yourself. Sometimes you may simply need to be a passive, listening friend.

However, these situations tend to be very rare, and it's even rarer that adopting an assertive communication style will have a negative impact.

Let's take a look at how some common situations can quickly go downhill when you use the other styles:

Making A Complaint
Passive communicators tend to be seen as a *'pushover.'* So, if you're making a complaint about poor service, a passive

communicator is likely to remain unheard. An aggressive communicator may inflame a situation and appear unreasonable, making it unlikely that their complaint will be taken seriously. Of course, sometimes aggressive communicators appear to get whatever they want by shouting the loudest, but that's not always the case. They will often cause a person to become passive aggressive.

Passive aggressive people are likely to be sarcastic, again making the person you are speaking likely to shut off. You may get an apology, but you're unlikely to be taken seriously or effect any real change. Assertive communicators, on the other hand, can get their point across clearly and without being aggressive. They don't feel the need to apply softening language, but they also don't use inflammatory language. They remain clear, calm and focus on the facts at hand without becoming overly emotional.

This approach helps the person they are speaking to also remain calm, and actually listen to what the assertive communicator has to say.

When Discussing Promotion or Pay Rise At Work
Passive communicators are unlikely to raise these issues themselves. They may want to be considered for promotion or feel that they deserve a pay increase, but they rarely feel able to bring the subject up with their managers. This tends to mean that passive communicators get overlooked, or receive only the standard pay increases for their departments.

Aggressive communicators are much more likely to bring these issues to the table during a discussion, but their aggressive style can result in them not being taken seriously. In many cases, promotions involve managing others or handling bigger clients, and aggressive communicators could be seen as unsuitable for roles where diplomacy could be required.

Passive-aggressive communicators may raise issues like pay and promotions, but this is often indirectly, such as in the form of sarcastic comments about another person's success. This kind of approach is normally ignored by managers, or the passive-aggressive intent may be missed entirely. Either way, it rarely results in a positive outcome.

Assertive communicators raise these issues at the appropriate times. They also tend to have clear and succinct evidence to back up why they should be considered for a promotion or pay increase. By assertively stating their case, they make it easy for the manager to understand what is being requested, and why they should consider it. This approach is much more likely to be successful.

Discussing Relationship Issues
Passive communicators tend to shy away from raising relationship issues. At best they may give indirect hints as to how they would like something to change. They also find it very stressful when the other person directly raises issues. They may simply agree to another's points regardless of whether they actually believe them to be true. This can breed resentment both in the passive person because they feel frustrated or taken for granted, and in the other person who feels frustrated that they can't have an open and honest conversation.

Aggressive communicators may raise issues frequently, even when they may seem petty and small to the other person. They are also unlikely to accept any responsibility or fault themselves, and instead will list a catalog of complaints about their partner. The other person may feel upset or attacked by the aggressive communicator's style. They are likely to either walk away from the conversation, become passive-aggressive, or even become aggressive themselves.

Passive-aggressive communicators raise issues indirectly, in the form of unkind, off the cuff remarks. Sometimes, they will *'sit'* on the issue for a long time, and then seemingly lose their temper over what appears to be a small transgression. They may also respond to criticism with a sarcastic front. The other person is likely to find their comments irritating, and may even fail to notice them. This leaves the passive aggressive person feeling even more frustrated.

Assertive communicators raise relationship issues in a timely manner and take care not to use blaming language. By calmly pointing out how they feel, and what made them feel that way, the other person is better able to listen and respond without becoming defensive. Assertive communicators are also able to take responsibility for their own part in a relationship issue and take care to acknowledge both sides of an argument.

Telling Somebody 'No.'
Passive communicators almost never tell anybody *'no.'* In an effort to avoid confrontation, they will take on almost any task or request, sometimes to the detriment of their own health or responsibilities. When this happens, the passive person may become so frustrated that they begin to display passive-aggressive behaviors.

Aggressive communicators have no problem telling people *'no.'* They often don't feel the need to offer an explanation, even if the request made of them is quite reasonable. This can lead to them damaging relationships and burning bridges.

Passive-aggressive communicators also struggle to say *'no.'* Unlike the passive communicator, they won't accept the request good-naturedly. They may mutter under their breath, or agree to do it with a short, sharp **'fine.'** They may say *'yes,'* but their body language and actions are often showing extreme reluctance. They may even agree to do something only to purposely do it badly, or pretend to forget to do it all.

Assertive people have no problem saying *'no.'* Unlike aggressive communicators, assertive people will normally respond to a reasonable request with a good reason, or even a counter-proposal. For example, if asked to attend a last-minute meeting, an assertive communicator might say *"I can't attend tonight as I have a prior appointment but if you have the date for the next meeting I can make sure I'm available."* If they deem a request unreasonable, an assertive communicator is happy to simply say no without an explanation, but they don't resort to aggressive communication styles.

The Power of Assertiveness

Being assertive means being able to stand up for your rights, or the rights of others in a calm and confident way. It's normal to adopt a passive or aggressive style sometimes, but the aim should be to remain assertive as often as possible. Sometimes assertiveness is confused with aggression, or with being *'bossy,'* but that's not true assertiveness. Assertiveness is simply a matter of getting your point across without causing others to become upset, or becoming upset yourself.

Being assertive means being able to express your thoughts and feelings in a direct, honest and appropriate way. If you've recognized yourself as an aggressive, passive, or passive-aggressive communicator naturally, then you may worry that you simply aren't assertive and can't experience the benefits of this communication style.

It's important to recognize that assertiveness is a skill, not a personality trait. It's a very valuable skill that allows you to communicate better on every level. You can learn to be assertive in the same way you learn any new skill. Through study and practice, you can become more assertive over time.

Another important thing is to understand what assertiveness is, and isn't. Being assertive doesn't mean disregarding the thoughts and feelings of others. In fact, being assertive means always respecting other people's thoughts, feelings, and beliefs as well as your own. You can be an assertive communicator without resorting to being rude or aggressive. Instead, assertiveness is stating your expectations clearly and ensuring that your rights and the rights of others are considered.

Assertiveness is also about encouraging others to also be open and honest about their views, and respecting these, actively taking them into consideration. Assertive communicators listen respectfully to the views and opinions of others, regardless of if they are in agreement with them. They are also able to accept responsibility for their own mistakes or misunderstandings and are able to openly apologize when appropriate.

How To Start To Be More Assertive Immediately

Here are some quick tips on how to start being assertive today! Start with just one of them, and make it your focus. Once it becomes a habit, implement another one. Before you know it, you'll be communicating assertively under most circumstances!

Don't Try To Control Other People

Assertive people know that they can only control their own behavior and not that of others. In fact, assertiveness is all about self-control. Assertive people control their emotions and keep their reactions in check. They make clear their position and then let the other person choose how to react to that information.

Next time you are having a difficult conversation, try stating your expectations calmly and clearly, and not trying to control the other person's reaction or behavior.

Use 'I' Statements

Assertive people use *'I'* statements instead of blaming others for how they feel. The next time somebody does something that upsets you, try using an *'I'* statement. So instead of *saying 'you shouldn't have gone to the party without me,'* try saying *'I was upset when I realized that you went to the party without me.'*

Doing this allows you to take responsibility for your feelings, while still addressing the issue with the other person. When the blame is removed, the other person can respond in a more calm and appropriate manner.

Ask For Time To Think If You Need It

Assertive people don't magically have all the right answers and responses in the heat of discussion. However, they recognize when they may need more time to think or reconsider their position. And when that happens, they are confident in asking for the time to think.

If you find yourself feeling anxious that you don't have the right thing to say, simply calmly ask for time to think. You can use phrases *like "That's a great question/point, I'd like some time to consider it, I'll come back to you this afternoon with my thoughts." Or "I'll need to think about that. When's a good time for us to pick this conversation back up?"*

Listen Carefully to The Other Person
This is something we'll cover in more detail in the next chapter, but it's important that you really listen to the other person's point of view. Remember, that being assertive means considering the other person's opinions and beliefs. You can't consider them if you aren't listening.

When the other person is speaking, give them your full attention. Don't interrupt, fidget, or otherwise detract from what they are saying. Simply take in the information they are giving you as calmly as you possibly can.

Recognize That Sometimes You Have to Agree To Disagree
Being assertive is about getting your points heard, and standing up for your rights. It's not about winning every argument or talking everybody around to your point of view. Of course, the ideal result is that others agree with your thoughts and opinions, but if they don't then you need to recognize when it's time to agree to disagree.

Address Specific Behaviors

When raising an issue, try and focus on the specific behavior that you want the other person to address. By doing this, you make it feel less like a personal attack to which the other person has to respond in defense. Instead, they can respond more calmly

Avoid the temptation to try and make the other person feel guilty, and use 'I' statements where possible. Remain calm, and try to avoid overt displays of emotion such as crying.

Respect Your Own Self-Worth

Assertive people know their worth. They can hold their own in a conversation because they know that the other person's opinion of them does not define them as a person. They don't back down out of fear of rejection because they know they are worth more than that.

If you struggle to be assertive because of a lack of self-worth, take some steps to build your own self-esteem. Take time to reflect regularly on things you have done well that day, and on your positive qualities.

The Benefits of Being Assertive

Being assertive offers many benefits. Learning to be more assertive can help you to effectively express your feelings in a way that others can understand, without emotional charge. It allows you to be clear about what your needs are so that others are able to meet them. It also helps you keep people from taking advantage of you, and ensures that your opinions are heard. Behaving assertively can help you gain the respect of others, and in turn, improve your own confidence and self-esteem.

It can also help you to strengthen existing personal relationships by being open and honest, and listening carefully to the other person's concerns.

Assertive people are often more successful people. This is at least in part down to the fact that they are able to clearly articulate their ideas and ambitions in an appropriate way. Communication skills are essential for success, and assertive communication is a vital skill to have for success.

Real Life Case Study of Assertive Communication

Mark works for a large accountancy firm in the administration department. Mark is hard working and efficient and always completes his tasks within the deadlines he is given. Because of this, he frequently finds that certain colleagues ask him to do their tasks when they are running behind. While Mark can easily finish his own tasks on time, he doesn't have enough time to complete the tasks for others without staying late or getting in early.

Mark is naturally a passive communicator. He finds it difficult to say 'no' to his colleagues because he does not want to appear rude or to cause any confrontation. However, taking on so much extra work because he was unable to say no meant that he couldn't complete his own workload in normal working hours. His stress levels began to rise as a result.

With the increasing stress came increasing resentment. Mark felt that his colleagues were taking advantage of him, but he lacked the confidence to tell them this or to refuse the extra work. As a result, Mark was left feeling frustrated because his colleagues continued to expect him to pick up their work. Over time the stress became so high that Mark was forced to take time off work with stress-related illness, and his doctor referred him to a trained therapist. During his sessions, Mark discussed with his therapist how he often feels unable to say 'no' and how this effectively leaves him feeling powerless and taken for granted.

By always saying *'yes,'* Mark was avoiding having to deal with any confrontation, but in the long run, the damage to his health and self-esteem wasn't worth the cost.

Mark's therapist helped him to see that by changing his communication style, he could say *'no'* while still minimizing the chance of conflict. By adopting an assertive communication style, Mark would be able to more clearly express his own needs to his colleagues and avoid feeling like he was being taken advantage of.

After working on his assertiveness, Mark learned that saying *'no'* isn't rude, it's sometimes essential. He felt more able to articulate to his colleagues that it wasn't fair of them to shift their own responsibilities onto him.

When Mark returned to work, he felt much more able to refuse to take on other people's responsibilities while still being polite and reasonable. He found that when he applied his learnings to his conversations at work, he didn't feel guilty for saying no. He didn't cause any confrontation because he was better able to express why he couldn't help.

With his new ability to be assertive, Mark was able to concentrate on his own work and speak to his manager about taking on his own small additional responsibilities. This ensured that he would get the credit for any additional work he did on top of his normal duties.

This allowed Mark to feel more empowered, and to gain additional experience that benefits his career.

It's true that a large part of having an assertive communication style is how, and what, you say. However, it's very difficult to say the right things in the right way if you're not listening to the other person.

In the next chapter, we'll take a look at how to improve your listening skills to become a better communicator.

Chapter 5 – The Vital Ingredient for Better Communication

"Seek first to understand, then to be understood."
Stephen Covey.

Hearing Vs. Listening

Listening is one of the most crucial aspects of communication – and it's one that a lot of us get wrong without even realizing it. How often have your thoughts drifted off while someone was speaking to you?

Perhaps you were thinking of a task you needed to do, or perhaps you were planning your response to them in your head while they were speaking. All too often, we're distracted while people are speaking. The distractions come from everywhere. A noisy environment, something troubling you, if the person speaking has a tic or some physical feature you find distracting, your own emotional response to their words... The list is endless.

Sure, you might still hear the words the person is saying. You might even be able to repeat them back verbatim as *'proof'* you were listening. Unfortunately, hearing isn't listening. Listening goes way beyond hearing the words and understanding their semantic meaning. The kind of listening that accompanies assertive communication is known as *'active'* listening.

Active listening is listening done right. It happens when you put these distractions to one side and focus only on the person speaking and what they are saying. You just listen, without adding your own viewpoint or applying judgment to what they are saying. It sounds simple, but it can be a difficult skill to master because it requires you to put your own personal feelings aside for a short while.

Active listeners not only hear what's being said, but they also notice the way the message is communicated. They are great at reading between the lines of a conversation because they pick up on all the verbal and non-verbal cues. These cues help you to understand the whole message the speaker is really trying to get across.

The benefits of active listening are huge when it comes to communicating. It helps you build trust, gets people to open up to you and can help avoid or resolve potential conflict.

In this chapter we'll look at techniques that you can implement to help you listen more actively.

Why We Get Distracted
It's generally thought that we only use 25% of our capacity to listen. More accurately, it only takes 25% of our brain function to listen to another person speak. The other 75% that isn't being used is what allows us to let our minds wander.

Part of the reason for this, is that we can think much faster than we can speak. So, when someone is speaking, our brain is thinking much faster than it hears their words. One tip to help you to focus is to repeat the words back in your head as the other person speaks. This will use up a little more brain capacity and force you to focus on what they are saying.

The rest of your attention should still be focused on the

person speaking, paying attention to their tone, body language and any non-verbal signals they are giving you. By focusing your attention on these things, you will be picking up on the whole message the person is trying to deliver – and not just the words they are saying.

Communication Barriers & How To Overcome Them

Every time we communicate with another person, there are numerous barriers between us. The aim of good communication is to remove those barriers so that we can hear the whole message the other person is communicating. Barriers can be physical barriers, like a noisy environment or a desk divider. Anything that makes it difficult to actually hear the person or see their body language is a barrier. But barriers can also be invisible, or internal.

If you've resolved not to listen to what someone has to say because you're sure you know what they're going to say already – that's a barrier. If you don't like a person, and you find yourself wanting to not agree with anything they say – that's another barrier.

Race, language and culture can all be barriers to effective communication. And while some –such as language – can be difficult to overcome just by listening, most of them can be removed if you're willing to make the effort.

Allowing prejudices to affect how you listen is doing both yourself, and the other person a huge disservice. It can affect your personal and professional relationships and hurts your ability to build real and meaningful connections.

Here are a few common barriers to active listening and communication that you may encounter:

Environmental Distractions – A noisy room, your cell phone, the TV playing in the background. Even the view from a window or the temperature in the room can be a barrier. These are all examples of environmental barriers that distract your attention. Multitasking is another environmental distraction. If you're trying to do something else at the same time as listening, chances are you won't be doing a great job at either the task or the listening.

You should try to remove as many of these barriers as you can. Switch off the TV, turn off or put away the cell phone. Sit so that you can't see out of the window, or wear layers if you know a meeting room or place has a lot of temperature fluctuations. Give the person speaking your full attention.

Of course, you can't remove them all the time. If there are barriers you can't remove, then you need to try your best to ignore them.

Assumptions
Most of us have heard the phrase that to assume *'makes an ass out of u and me.'* It's an amusing way to articulate the fact that assumptions are often unhelpful – especially when it comes to communicating with other people.

Because our minds work so much faster than the other person can speak, it can be tempting to analyze what's being said as you hear it. When you do that you might assume that you know what the other person is going to say next. While it's possible you're correct, you may also be wrong and this kind of assumption can lead to misunderstandings or even conflict.

Emotional Barriers

Pride, anxiety, fear, anger. Often the barriers to effective listening and communicating are emotional. Our emotions can cloud our judgment, lead us to make assumptions, and put us immediately on the defensive.

For example, if your spouse approaches you to discuss an issue, you may immediately become defensive and aggressive and try to deflect any issues back onto them. Or you may become quiet and withdrawn, desperate for the conversation to end so that you can return to normal. Both reactions are damaging to your communication and prevent you from listening properly.

When you listen with an open mind, and put aside your emotions, you can make real breakthroughs in both work and personal relationships. Of course, this is often easier said than done, but the reward is always worth the effort.

Instead of viewing criticisms, at work or at home, as personal attacks, view them as an opportunity for development. Even if you don't agree with the criticism or comment, it gives you a valuable insight into how someone else views you and the opportunity to influence that.

Gender Barriers

Men and women have a natural tendency to communicate in slightly different ways. Of course, this is a generalization and not all men or all women are typical. It's still worth bearing these differences in mind the next time you're communicating with each other. Men tend to be more direct and get right to the point. They use fewer words per day on average than women, and they are much less likely to use softening language. They are less emotive and descriptive and tend to have a more naturally commanding presence.

They often view communication as a means to an end – to get a point across, to solve a problem, etc.

Women are more descriptive and emotional. They tend to be better at showing empathy and talking about emotions, but they can lack authority and don't always get straight to the point. Women tend to view communication as a relationship building activity and are comfortable with conversation for the sake of conversation.

Neither style is 'correct' but understanding these common differences can help when you are communicating to someone of the opposite gender. By aiming to bridge the gap a little, you can have more meaningful and productive conversations.

Attitude
A word that's often used casually (and negatively) but your attitude is made up of many different influencing factors.

Your attitude towards another person can be made up of your past experiences with that person, your own beliefs and culture, and numerous other factors.

Often, our attitude is most positive towards people we perceive to be like ourselves, or like someone we aspire to be. This is where prejudices seep in if we don't actively guard against them. You may have prejudices towards people based on all kinds of factors: where they live, their skin color, their accent, their appearance, the school they attended, or their political leanings.

When we encounter someone who we perceive positively, we will be more likely to listen to and support their views and opinions. If we perceive them negatively, we are more likely to ignore or oppose their views and opinions.

Active listening means removing this barrier of attitude and letting go of the judgments we might be tempted to make about somebody. Doing this allows you to stop seeing the world purely from your own perspective, and put yourself in the shoes of someone else.

How To Become An Active Listener

We've looked at what active listening is not, and identified some barriers to active listening. But what exactly is active listening and how can you start to implement it in your conversations?

Active listening is listening with the genuine intention of understanding the message that someone else is communicating. Although the words they use are important, the message is usually more than just the words they say. Few people openly admit to everything they are thinking or feeling but picking up on the small clues they give can elevate your communication from good to great.

This is where active listening also involves observing the non-verbal messages that the other person is giving. What do their tone, body language, and facial expressions convey to you? Is there a discrepancy between what they say and their non-verbal cues?

Taking in the whole message in this way can help you respond in the most appropriate way. It can also put the other person at ease and make them feel respected. Giving someone your full, undivided attention while they speak is one of the best ways to demonstrate respect.

Tips for Active Listening

So, what changes can you start to make now in order to be a more active listener?

<u>Pay Close Attention</u>
There's a reason many of us aren't already great active listeners. It requires you to give the speaker all of your attention, and that's not something that comes naturally to us. However, it's a skill you need to learn if you want to develop your active listening.

It would be very difficult to give someone your full and undivided attention for an hour-long presentation. However, active listening is only necessary when you're having a face-to-face conversation with somebody. During a normal conversation, the other person is unlikely to speak for more than a couple of minutes before they expect you to respond.

So, while it may not come naturally at first, giving someone your full attention while they speak shouldn't be too difficult. Start small, and practice during short and casual conversations. For example when your colleague tells you about the TV show they started watching, or your spouse describes their day.

Give them your full attention while they speak. If you find your mind wandering, don't beat yourself up about it. Just redirect your attention back to the person speaking. The more you practice this, the more natural it will become during all conversations.

<u>Never Interrupt</u>

Resist the urge to interrupt while the other person is speaking. Even if they make a point that you believe is wrong, or they say something that you disagree with very strongly. If you jump in before allowing a person to speak, you don't get the whole context of their comments. Jumping in because of a word or phrase they used can make them feel attacked and lead to conflict.

Instead, come back to that point when they finish speaking. Perhaps ask them a genuine non-challenging question about the point that you don't agree with. When you understand why a person might think a certain way, it makes it easier to counter this with your own opinion.

Allow them to say everything they want to say before you speak – and they will be more likely to afford you the same respect.

Silence Your Thoughts/Opinions

When you are listening to another person, only their opinions are relevant, yours are not. We live in a world where people can freely express their opinions on multiple platforms, and what is always painfully apparent is that not everyone will agree with you.

Most of us have witnessed a heated *'discussion'* online between two people where the ubiquitous phrase *'I'm entitled to my opinion'* is used. It's true, we're all entitled to our own opinions, but sometimes we guard and defend them so vigorously that we don't allow ourselves to be open to or accept the opinions of others.

You don't have to agree with somebody to listen to them. You also don't need to make the point that your opinion is the opposite if there is nothing at stake. We're so used to airing our opinions and defending our entitlement that we sometimes forget that other people are entitled to disagree or simply not care about them.

Assertive communication is about being able to assert your opinion, but it's not about forcing it on others or disregarding their opinion. If you allow yourself to get distracted by your own opinions while the other person is still speaking, you lose the opportunity to learn something new. You also lose the chance to make a truly effective counter-argument if you do need to assert your own opinion.

It's always tempting to jump in and interrupt if somebody says something you don't agree with. But cutting them off and interrupting before they finish demonstrates a lack of respect – and they are likely to reward your impatience by not listening to your points anyway. Your conversation becomes less of an exchange and more a case of two people stating their opinions while neither is actually listening. At best, this kind of conversation will be over quickly. At worst it can turn into a high conflict situation.

The active listening part of assertive communication means that you need to be able to listen carefully to the other person's opinions and beliefs. Then you signal that you have heard and understood them. This is a crucial step in the process.

Assertive communicators don't assert their own opinion until they have listened to and understood the other person's opinion.

Observe Non-Verbal Cues
Pay close attention to the non-verbal cues that the other person is giving you. These are things like their tone of voice, the speed and pitch of their words, their facial

expressions and their body language.

All of us have experienced times when you've noticed that somebody's words don't match the non-verbal cues they are giving. For example, someone who says they are *'fine'* but their tone sounds angry, or their eyes appear watery. These are clear signs that what they are saying isn't the whole story.

Sometimes the cues are more subtle. Someone might avoid eye contact which could indicate they are hiding something – or just very shy. Perhaps they might glance at their watch which could indicate that for some reason they are concerned about the time and it would be better to reschedule the conversation.

Sometimes the cues people give are difficult to interpret, but you don't need to be a mind reader to understand what's going on. If you're unsure, simply wait for a pause in the conversation and ask them.

For example, if someone is constantly looking towards the door as they speak to you, ask them if they have somewhere else they need to be. It may be that actually, they are expecting another person to join you, or that they do, indeed have somewhere else to be.

Either way, most people will be happy to answer you and pleased that you are paying such close attention to them and their potential needs. Of course, the way you ask will make a difference. We'll take a look at how to ask questions in a moment.

Pause For Thought
I've mentioned that trying to formulate your response before the other person even finishes speaking is a bad

idea. But you do need to respond, and you do need time to consider that response.

When the other person finishes speaking, take a few seconds to collect your own thoughts before speaking. When you do speak, don't offer your opinion or response straight away. Instead, clarify your understanding of what the other person has just said, or ask questions in a non-challenging way.

Ask Questions
Your aim with active listening is to understand the whole message, and for the other person to recognize that they have been heard and understood.

Questions are a great way to clarify points, get someone to open up, and to demonstrate an interest in what a person is saying. Open questions like *"Tell me more about…"* will prompt more information than closed questions.

Of course, the way you ask a question makes a difference to how the other person will respond. Make sure to avoid wording questions in a way that seems challenging, and consider your own non-verbal cues.

For example, earlier we discussed how someone glancing towards the door a lot might have somewhere else they need to be. Asking them if this is the case can be either supportive or challenging depending on your own non-verbal cues.

If you ask with a frown, or a challenging tone, the other person will interpret that you are angry with them or are implying that they are being rude. If your body language is open, and your tone is kind and inquisitive, they will be more likely to correctly interpret your attempt to establish if the discussion needs rescheduling.

Pay Attention To Your Own Non-Verbal Cues
You should try and be aware of the signals you are sending to the other person as they speak. For example, if you're not looking at them and are instead gazing out of the window, you will appear disinterested.

If you frown, purse your lips or sigh as they speak, it will appear that you do not agree with what they are saying. Remember that one of the goals of assertive communication and active listening is to allow the other person to air their own views without judgment.

Nodding from time to time, or giving a quick murmur of agreement helps the other person to feel confident that they are being listened to.

Summarize What They Say
When they finish speaking, paraphrase in your own words what you believe their message to be. For example, a colleague might complain about their boss giving them instructions for a task, and then not approving the outcome despite following the instructions given.

In this situation, you might say something like: *"So, you're annoyed because you don't think the instructions he gave were clear enough for you to do the task the way he really wanted? And that meant you wasted a lot of time that could have been avoided with better instructions?"*

By doing this, you're reflecting their message back to them as you understood it, and allowing them to either confirm your understanding or to give more detail. Paraphrasing removes the possibility of misunderstandings and allows any obvious misunderstandings to be addressed quickly.

It also demonstrates to the other person that they have been heard, which is basically what everyone really wants when they are communicating.

Active listening isn't always easy – but it is always worth it. If you can apply the techniques in this chapter to your conversations with others, you'll find that they respond to you in a much more positive way than ever before.

It won't happen overnight, and you'll need some practice before it becomes natural but even just small changes to the way you listen can have a big impact.

We've discussed paying attention to body language several times in this chapter, but how do you accurately read someone else's body language?

Let's take a look in more depth at body language in the next chapter.

Chapter 6 – The Incredible Power of *EFFECTIVE* Body Language

"Body language and tone of voice - not words - are our most powerful assessment tools."
Christopher Voss.

Communicating Through Body Language

Body language is incredibly important in communication. When you understand how to read body language, and the subconscious signals you send to others via your own body language, you can more easily manage the outcome of a conversation. Body language is an outward signal of someone's internal emotions, so it's a great skill to be able to read it accurately. Imagine how useful it would be to know when someone isn't being totally honest. Or being able to tell when someone is genuinely interested in what you're saying or is just being polite. Mind reading isn't really possible, but understanding body language gives you a huge insight into what others may be thinking or feeling.

Have you ever come across somebody who seemed very perceptive? Chances are that they were very good at reading body language. Sometimes this is a natural talent, but it can be a learned skill that anyone can develop. By applying the information in this chapter to your real-life conversations, you'll soon find that you are beginning to understand people much better.

Of course, the hints and tips we give here are generic and based mostly on the English-speaking western world. Everybody will have subtle differences to their own body language which will be relevant to their culture, upbringing, and their own personal experiences. However, an understanding of the key elements of body language will still give you incredible insight into other people.

Key Body Language Signals

Body language is a vast topic – one that could easily take up its own book! In this chapter, we'll cover some of the key signals that others are likely to be transmitting during conversations. We'll also look at how you can make simple changes to your own body language to project a more confident and assertive persona.

Let's take a look at some common body language that signals different emotions.

Nervous Body Language

If you want to project a more confident image, avoiding some of these common tell-tale signs of nerves can help. If someone you are speaking to is displaying these signs, try and take steps to make them more comfortable.

Adjusting Clothing Repeatedly –For example, adjusting a tie, smoothing down a skirt, picking lint from clothing. This can be a sign that they feel nervous about their appearance in particular.

Fidgeting – For example, tapping a foot repeatedly, playing with an object, repeatedly clicking a biro.

Clenched Hands – This can indicate either negativity to what is being said, or it can indicate anxiety more generally. Pay attention to the other signals and the context of a conversation to decide which is being displayed.

Tense Muscles – When someone is afraid, their muscles may tense in readiness for the *'fight or flight response.'*

Perspiration – This can occur as part of a milder nervous reaction, but if someone is visibly perspiring and the room temperature is low, they are potentially feeling very anxious.

Arms Folded, Shoulders Hunched – This is a defensive stance, indicating that the person is subconsciously expecting an attack of some kind. The *'attack'* could be verbal or just an unpleasant conversation.

Some of these nervous behaviors can be irritating and distracting to others. For example, repeatedly clicking a biro generates a sound that can irritate people trying to speak or listen. If you encounter somebody doing this while you speak, understanding that they are probably nervous may help you to be less irritated. Try and get them to relax a little to stop them from repeating the behavior. Or find an excuse to politely ask to borrow their pen!

Depending on the intensity, sometimes these signals convey more than mere nerves. Displaying a lot of these signals, or displaying them very obviously can indicate that someone is genuinely afraid. This can mean they are experiencing more than the mild kind of social or performance anxiety that we associate with nervous behavior.

Of course, depending on the level of their personal anxiety, someone may display these symptoms intensely in a normal social setting. You may also see them if someone has a phobia and is in a setting that is beginning to trigger it. For example, a claustrophobic person in an elevator.

Confident Body Language

These signals show that someone is feeling confident. These are the body language signals that you would expect to see from assertive communicators. By consciously adopting some of these signals when you are speaking, you will automatically come across as more confident and assertive – even if you're not feeling it.

Rubbing The Palms Together – When someone rubs their palms together, it's a positive sign. It may indicate excitement about the topic they are speaking about, or that they expect a positive outcome to a particular matter.

Smiling – A true smile shows the teeth and affects the eyes – usually creating tiny wrinkles at the corners of the eyes and the eyebrows come slightly down. Closed-lipped smiles, or smiles that don't affect the eyes are unlikely to be genuine.

Leaning Forward When Speaking – This tends to show interest and is usually done by the speaker in a way that makes the listeners feel as though something secret and interesting is being shared. When the speaker does it, if the audience is interested they will normally lean forward as well, eager to hear the information.

Shoulders Back And Relaxed, Chin Parallel To The Floor – This indicates that someone is comfortable in their own skin and feels that they belong. They aren't inviting attention, but they aren't trying to deflect it either. Adopting this posture is a quick way to appear instantly more confident.

Aggressive Body Language

These body language signals indicate that somebody is feeling angry and that the conversation may be about to take a turn for the worse. When you spot signals like these, you'll need to decide the best way to respond depending on the situation.

In many situations, especially work situations, the appropriate response is not to become aggressive yourself. Sometimes the best solution will be to end the conversation as quickly as possible and excuse yourself. Other times you may need to adopt a passive style and submissive body language if it is important to calm the person down quickly.

Handling aggression is a tricky subject as the right response depends on many variables. However, when you understand the body language signals associated with aggression you can take action more quickly. You'll be able to either calm the situation or remove yourself from it before it becomes outright hostile.

Standing Too Close – When people invade your personal space, it's often a sign of aggression designed to make you feel intimidated. It can also be a sign of flirtation, but the context and other signals should make it clear which is happening.

Widened Stance – When trying to appear intimidating, people often stand with their feet wider and their hands on their hips. It's a subconscious gesture designed to make them appear larger and more threatening.

Pointing A Finger – When someone points or wags a finger while speaking, it's usually a sign that they're getting hot under the collar about something.

Banging A Fist On The Desk – This is a pretty obvious one, but people will often do this when they're passionate about something and feel that others aren't hearing them or don't understand.

Wild Hand Gestures – These can indicate either high levels of excitement about a topic or anger/aggression.

Superior Body Language

These signals indicate that somebody is feeling superior to the other people in the group. They can sometimes be confused for signals of confidence, but they tend to be over-confident rather than the relaxed and easy-going confidence that most of us prefer to project.

They can indicate a level of arrogance, and if the person you are speaking to displays these signs then they may be considering themselves better than you. It's easy to take offense at this, but understanding these signals can be very helpful when you need to charm somebody.

If you can see that they feel superior, feeding into this in subtle ways can warm them to you. Watch carefully for signs of how exactly they feel superior. For example, if they puff up their chest every time they talk about golf, compliment them on their golfing technique and ask if they can give you any tips.

Hands In A 'Steeple' Gesture Below The Chin Or In Front Of The Face – This usually occurs when people are sat down, elbows resting on a table. It can indicate that the listener feels like the speaker needs something from them. It can make you appear arrogant, so it should be avoided when you need to persuade somebody. If stood up, the steeple gesture is sometimes used in an almost 'pointing' way while addressing an audience.

Arms Folded, With Thumbs Pointing Upwards – Arms folded is always a negative sign, but when the thumbs are displayed upwards, it also adds an indication that the other person views themselves as superior.

Chin Tilted Upwards – This may be ever so slight but indicates they are 'looking down' at the speaker.

Flirtatious Body Language
These signals indicate that somebody is flirting with another person and is wanting attention.

Smiling – When it appears in conjunction with several other signals, a smile can indicate that someone is flirting with you. We want to appear happy and attractive to people who we find attractive, and a smile is the easiest way to do this. Women often turn their head sideways and look up at the person they are flirting with while smiling.

Face Resting On The Backs Of The Hands, Fingers Lightly Intertwined And Elbows Resting On A Table – Most often used by women, this indicates that the person is open to receiving compliments from you.

Moistening Of The Lips – Can also be a nervous signal, but in conjunction with other signals like smiling or touching it can be flirtatious.

Touching The Other Person – Briefly touching someone, for example, a hand on the arm or the shoulder, signifies a sexual interest.

Smoothing Their Hair – This is a kind of *'preening'* gesture that indicates that the other person wants you to find them attractive.

Holding Eye Contact For Longer Than Usual – Most of the time we don't hold full eye contact for more than a few seconds. We'll discuss this further later on in this chapter. When eye contact is held a little longer than usual, it can indicate flirtation. It can also be a sign of aggression, but the accompanying signals should make it clear which is occurring!

Disagreeing Body Language
These signals indicate that somebody is disagreeing with what they are hearing, or they are critical of it.

A Hand Held To The Cheek, One Finger Resting On Or Close To The Mouth And The Index Finger Against The Cheek Pointed Up Towards The Hairline – This looks a little like an 'L' shape.

Face Tilted Down, Chin Towards The Chest – so that they are looking up at the speaker.

One Or Both Arms Crossed Tightly Over The Body – Arms folded is usually a negative gesture, but the way the arms are folded can indicate different emotions. If the person's hands are resting on their upper arms just above the elbow, palms pressed down, then they are probably disagreeing with what is being said.

Legs Tightly Crossed – In a similar manner to the arms-crossed gesture, if somebody has their legs crossed tightly, it can indicate that they don't agree with what they are hearing.

Elbows Resting On The Table, Hands Clenched – This signifies a negative attitude to what is being discussed. The hands might be low, close to the person's waist, or they could be below the chin. The higher the hands are raised, the more likely it is that they are disagreeing. Watch for whitening of the knuckles. When the hands are clenched tightly so that the knuckles are white, it's a clearer sign of negativity.

It can also be anxiety, so take the context of the conversation into account. For example, displayed by a candidate in a job interview this gesture is more likely to be nerves. Displayed by the interviewer, it could be that they don't like the answers being given!

Dishonest Body Language

These signals indicate that somebody isn't being completely honest with what they are saying. It could be an outright lie, or more a case of selectively leaving out details that they don't want you to know. If somebody is displaying these signals, don't take what they say at face value.

Touching or Covering Their Mouth – during or straight after speaking.

Touching Their Nose – during or straight after speaking.

Tugging At Their Collar.

Their Palms Are Hidden, Or They Are Concealing Their Hands – perhaps placed behind their back or in their pockets. Conversely, open palm gestures and openly displaying the hands can be interpreted as a sign of honesty.

Frequently Swallowing – If somebody's swallowing is very frequent, it could be a sign of lying.

Body Language Summary

These signals are all great ways of identifying another person's emotions, but they are more accurate indicators when they occur together.

Take the example of a woman smoothing down her skirt. Done repeatedly, it can indicate nervousness. Once or twice it may simply be that she likes the feel of the material. Or perhaps the skirt has a tendency to shift up when she moves, and she's just putting it back in place. A man flaring his nostrils might simply be unconsciously reacting to a pleasant or unpleasant smell rather than displaying signs of anger or aggression. Someone covering their mouth a lot may have anxiety about their breath, and so on.

Pay attention to their tone, stance, facial expression, and other body language signals before deciding what the signals are showing you. Focusing on one signal in isolation can give you the wrong interpretation. Of course, if you're already a little nervous in conversation, trying to read body language as well as keeping your cool and active listening can be a huge task. It may even initially distract you during conversations. To avoid this, try and get into the habit of reading body language all of the time – this way it's more of a background *'intuition'* than something distracting you.

Make a conscious effort the next time you're in a public place to discretely watch the people around you and try to identify their body language signals. You can do this on the bus, in café's, while walking down the street. The more you practice, the more natural and automatic it will become. You can even watch the body language on interview shows to see if you can spot any inconsistencies between what people say and what they might be feeling. You can spot body language signals on any television shows or movies, especially with the volume down. However, the obviously staged nature of these means how true to life and unexaggerated they are will depend on the quality of the acting.

Facial Expressions and Eye Contact
Facial expressions and eye signals also fall under the banner of body language. There is a wide range of signals that people can send with their facial expressions and eye movements. Some are much easier to read than others.

For example, most of us know that a smile is usually a good sign. Yet there are lots of other, subtler signals that we send with our facial expressions.

Most of us are pretty adept at reading basic facial expressions. Smiles, frowns, and raised eyebrows are normally fairly clear in what they are expressing. If you're trying to project a particular image to others, being aware of your facial expressions is a great place to start.

Here are some facial expressions and eye signals that convey particular emotions:

Smiling – A relaxed, genuine smile indicates someone is listening and interested in what is being said.

Yawning – Yawning can show that someone isn't interested, but it can also simply mean that they had a late night! Try not to be too offended if someone yawns while you're speaking, but watch out for other signs that you're losing their interest.

Staring Into Space Or Out Of A Window – If someone is staring intently at a point in the distance, it usually indicates that their mind is wandering. It could be that they're thinking carefully about the last point you made, but either way, they are no longer paying much attention to you. They could still be hearing the words, but they aren't really listening.

Flared Nostrils – This is the lizard brain preparing for fight or flight, allowing in more oxygen for the expected activity. Like sneering, it can indicate fear, anger, or irritation in humans.

Sneering – typically a warning of a potential attack in animals. Even though we don't bite, we still use this one. In humans tends to indicate either anger or irritation.

Corners of The Mouth Turned Down – This can potentially indicate several negative emotions like despair, unhappiness or anger, so pay close attention to the other signals being given.

Clenched Jaw – This is often a sign of barely-concealed anger.

Tight-Lipped Smile, Or Corners of The Mouth Drawn Down – This can indicate that someone is feeling negative about what is being said, or the person speaking. A tight-lipped smile can also indicate that someone is withholding information.

Wide Eyes – These can indicate surprise, shock or anxiety.

A sudden widening of the eyes tends to indicate shock, whereas if their eyes are generally wide and they look away a lot, it could be nerves or anxiety.

Eyes Darting Around – This can also indicate nerves if somebody is looking around constantly.

Getting Eye Contact Right

Eye contact is important, and your eyes project a lot of non-verbal signals to other people. Even slight movements of the eyes can signal your emotions. Some of these you will be completely unable to control.

For example, dilated pupils can indicate desire. It's often a sign of sexual attraction, but the same response also happens when you're hungry and finally get a meal you've been waiting a long time for! Steady eye contact is one of the best ways to appear assertive and confident. If you are reluctant to make eye contact at all, you will come across as nervous, or even a little shady depending on the rest of your body language.

Of course, hold eye contact too long, and you may be mistaken for being aggressive or flirtatious! But how long is too long?

An interesting study by *University College London* showed that the average length of eye contact tolerated from strangers is 3.2 seconds. Participants were happier with longer eye contact from people they were familiar with, but more than about 4-5 seconds can start to make people feel uncomfortable.

Most of us will instinctively lower our eyes before it continues too long. Normally, during a conversation, our gaze moves briefly to a different area of the face before returning to the eyes again for another few seconds.

Case Study – A Story of Body Language In A Job Interview

It's often said that in a job interview, the interviewer already has an idea of whether or not they will hire you in the first minute or two. A lot of this is based upon your appearance and your body language. Even if they don't realize it, the interviewer is assessing your body language when you arrive and while you speak. Displaying the right body language can be the difference between getting the job or not. The Head of Marketing at a mid-sized company interviewed two final candidates for a key role in Marketing. The first one, James, had five years' experience in a similar role, a college degree in Marketing and arrived for the interview dressed appropriately in a smart suit and tie.

The second candidate, John, had similar experience, a college degree in Marketing and also arrived dressed appropriately in a smart suit and tie. Given their similar experience at other companies, they gave remarkably similar responses to the key interview questions. Both clearly knew their stuff, and it should have been a very difficult decision, but after both interviews, the Head of Marketing knew exactly which candidate he wanted to hire.

James' body language had been nervous and submissive from the moment he arrived. When responding to some questions, his nervous behaviors like fidgeting were so pronounced it made him appear almost dishonest. The interviewer liked some of the answers he gave, but couldn't imagine him coping well in high-pressure meetings or handling tight deadlines.

John's body language had been calm and confident. While he did naturally display a couple of mild nervous behaviors like adjusting his tie, his overall demeanor projected confidence and assertiveness which gave the interviewer more trust in the responses he was giving. It allowed the interviewer to imagine him coping well with the demanding deadlines of the role.

The core skills an interviewer is looking for will vary depending on the job, and so too will the personal traits. However, taking care to appear relaxed and confident without accidentally coming across as arrogant will always stand you in good stead for a job interview.

So, if you want to create a good impression with others, pay attention to your body language. And if in doubt, smile! It's true that not all smiles are genuine, and it may sound contradictory to tell you to fake a smile if you're not really feeling it. However, a lot of people can't easily tell the difference. Especially if you put enough effort in to allow it to affect your eyes.

Smiling not only makes you seem approachable and friendly, relaxing others, it also actually tricks your brain into making you feel happier and more relaxed. So, fake it till you make it if you have to. A smile is pretty much always a good idea.

The next part of the book looks at the different types of communication – public speaking and presenting, conversing, formal communications such as job interviews or complaining to a company. We'll explore how the basics of listening and body language still apply, but how you should adapt your style slightly to fit the situation.

Chapter 7 – Become A Better Verbal Communicator

"The human brain starts working the moment you are born and never stops... until you stand up to speak in public."
George Jessel

Verbal Communication Skills

Public speaking is an activity that gives even the most confident among us a touch of butterflies. Most people list public speaking as one of their biggest fears and even people who regularly speak in public admit to being nervous beforehand. If you're in any way nervous about normal conversation, then the very idea of public speaking can be truly terrifying. But public speaking is a great skill to have, and successfully delivering a speech or presentation is an amazing confidence boost.

Just like conversational skills, public speaking skills can be learned, and anyone can do it. In this chapter, we'll look at the similarities and differences between public speaking and conversation, and how to nail public speaking even if you're not confident.

Public Speaking Vs. Conversing
Public speaking can be addressing a small audience in a meeting, delivering a presentation or even giving a speech at a wedding. Any time that you need to address an audience about a specific topic, that's public speaking. There are some major similarities and differences between conversing and public speaking, so let's take a look at some of them.

Conversation tends to be more two-way than public speaking, and it doesn't have to serve a specific purpose. Normally conversations are more social and relaxed than public speaking, and the focus is rarely on one person for longer than a minute or two. Of course, some conversations like a one to one meeting with your manager about your work performance can be just as focused and intense as public speaking!

Conversations are unlikely to be pre-rehearsed. While you can practice certain topics of conversation beforehand to help ease your nerves, it's very difficult to predict which way a conversation may go. Whether it's a business conversation or a personal conversation, there are always other people involved that can direct the conversation in a direction that you didn't anticipate.

When public speaking, you are in control of what is said. If you will be opening the floor to questions at the end of your speech presentation, there is a small chance you will get questions you are not prepared for. However, these can often be much more easily dealt with than a private conversation that gets derailed. We'll cover how to handle difficult questions after a presentation later in this chapter.

In both public speaking and conversations, silence is something that people tend to want to avoid. However, small periods of silence are a useful tool to allow other speakers or your audience to reflect on what has just been said. When you're public speaking, silences may feel as though they stretch out for much longer than they actually do. Which can lead to a tendency for you to avoid silence at all costs.

In fact, strategic silences are good to keep or regain your audience's interest. A strategic pause for thought, or to allow your audience to *'catch up'* can work very well as long as it's only a few seconds. In conversations, silences can be a great way to get somebody else to provide additional information. Most of us find silences unnerving and will rush to fill them so they can come in very handy indeed when you want somebody to open up. Doing this too often can be intimidating or irritating to the other person, however, so use them judiciously.

Humor is another tool that is useful in both public speaking and conversations. Of course, it's always important to make sure that the humor is appropriate. The kind of humor that you might use among a small circle of very close friends is usually different to what you would use with a group of your colleagues. If all eyes are on you, the impact of a badly-judged joke is much bigger. Only use humor if you're sure it will appeal to your audience. Used correctly, humor can add spark to a speech or presentation.

Both public speaking and conversation also rely heavily on tone of voice and body language to ensure that your message is delivered and understood as you intended. When you are public speaking, your body language can be particularly pronounced because your nerves are likely to be greater than in a regular conversation. You're also more likely to be consciously aware of your body language while public speaking. In some ways, this gives you a fantastic opportunity to address any signals or gestures that might confuse or distract your audience.

In the last chapter, we discussed in some detail how to use body language to come across as a confident and assertive speaker. These tips are as relevant in public speaking as they are for conversational speaking. Remember, pulling your shoulders back and keeping your chin parallel to the floor will help you appear more confident immediately.

Avoid any obvious nervous gestures like fidgeting.

Hands are often an issue for public speakers. When a whole room of people is looking at you, for some reason most of us become very aware of what we're doing with our hands. If you're naturally a gesticulator, try to make sure that you aren't over exaggerating the gestures when you speak, as this can really distract your audience. Also, remember that open palm gestures that reveal the palms of your hands are more likely to make you appear honest open and genuine. Hiding your palms in any way such as clenching your fists, putting your hands behind your back, having arms folded, will make you appear more defensive and potentially less genuine.

Public Speaking

The two basic types of public speaking are delivering a presentation and delivering a speech. There's a lot of overlap, but there are also some distinct differences and ways to deliver these. Let's take a look at some key presentation and speech delivery skills.

Presenting Skills

Presentations are a type of public speaking that are usually backed up by a series of slides. These are very common in business, and most office workers have heard or used the phrase 'death by PowerPoint' more than once. So, if you've been asked to give a presentation, you might be worried that people will automatically find it boring!

The purpose of a presentation is normally to inform or to persuade the audience. It could be an important piece of training or a sales pitch, but some key similarities apply. If you've been asked to do a presentation, keep these tips in mind.

The great thing about presentations vs. speeches is that you have your slides to give you a prompt about what you want to say. However, it's important to resist the temptation to cram everything you want to say onto the slides and then simply read from them. That's the worst kind of *'death by PowerPoint.'*

The slides should be concise, and as visually appealing as possible. If you have data to present, colorful and easy to read graphs can help drive the information home for the audience. Any text should only summarize key points, and your role as the speaker is to explain and expand upon those points in a way that engages the audience.

Don't be afraid to use notes, but these should be as concise as possible. Writing down your whole presentation and attempting to read it back is likely to result in you making little to no eye contact with anyone in the audience. Not to mention a stilted *'performance.'* Your notes should simply be prompts that go a little more in-depth than your slides so that you can refer to them if needed. Ideally, you will be able to talk through the slides while looking at your audience. In the same way, that eye contact keeps people engaged in regular conversations, your audience will be more engaged with you if you're actually looking at them.

If you're delivering information on a big topic, try and keep it concise and don't overwhelm your audience. Even if you have a huge breadth of knowledge on a topic, most people can't take in too much information at once. It's always better to concentrate on 3-4 key points in a little more depth than to try to cover ten points in one presentation. If you absolutely have to cover a lot of points, keep them as brief as you can by delivering only the key information about them.

Always try and have time for questions. If you're not a confident public speaker, ask the audience to save questions until the end, and invite them after you finish to ask their questions. If you're an accomplished speaker, you may be comfortable accepting questions throughout. This approach can help keep the audience interested, but it can also sometimes derail your presentation. Depending on the questions, it can take you and the audience off on a tangent before you've addressed your key points.

Saving questions to the end helps you maintain the structure of your presentation. It also avoids people asking questions that you would have covered on the next slide before you're ready to discuss that material.

Delivering A Speech
A speech is usually motivational, personal, or persuasive. It might be a political speech, a wedding speech or telling *'your story'* at a dinner or an event. Speeches don't normally use slides or visual aids, and so you'll need to rely solely on charisma to keep your audience listening. Because all eyes will be on you – and not your visual aids – body language is absolutely crucial. Make sure you are displaying confident, open body language while you speak.

Normally people in attendance at a speech are keen to hear the speaker, so you're starting on the right note before you even speak. However, most people can't listen along for more than twenty minutes without becoming distracted. Keep your speech short and sweet and under twenty minutes if you can.

Understanding your audience is important in delivering a

great speech. Delivering the best man's speech will be different from addressing the local book club. Understanding your audience and what they're expecting from you will help you prepare and deliver a killer speech. When you understand the audience you're addressing, you'll be able to tailor the speech to keep them interested and engaged.

It's better not to use notes if you can help it. You want people to connect with you, and to do that you will need to be looking at your audience, and not down at your notes. Practicing regularly before you deliver your speech will help and don't get hung up on getting it word-for-word perfect. As long as you get your main points across and it sounds natural, your audience will love it.

There are sometimes occasions where the lines are blurred. For example, a best man might deliver a speech backed up by a PowerPoint presentation, or a CEO might deliver a presentation without any actual slides. With this in mind, we'll move on to look at some more general tips on public speaking that will apply no matter what the occasion.

General Tips on How To Deliver When Public Speaking

Whether you've got a speech or a presentation to deliver, feeling anxious before public speaking is natural. The trick is to funnel all that nervous energy into delivering a great speech or presentation. Here are some tips that apply to any kind of public speaking.

Preparation

Always remember the five 'P's. *Proper. Preparation. Prevents. Poor. Performance.*

This philosophy can be applied to most things, but it's especially true with public speaking. Over time, as your confidence grows, you might be able to pick up a last-minute presentation or speech with ease. Yet even when you're an experienced speaker, it's the preparation that really makes your public speaking appear polished.

Make sure you have enough time to prepare. Write out what you want to say, and then read it aloud. We tend to write a little differently than we speak, so if it sounds unnatural when you read it aloud, tweak the wording until you feel more natural.

Once you have the *'perfect'* script, you need to try and learn it. You can do this by repeating it often enough that you can start to recite it by heart. One way to speed this up – especially if you don't live alone and feel ridiculous talking aloud to yourself all the time – is to record yourself.

You don't have to video record at this stage. Simply record the audio of you delivering the script. Once you have a recording where you feel it sounds good enough, play this back to yourself whenever you have a minute. Listening to yourself deliver the speech or presentation repeatedly will help you to memorize it. Don't worry if you never memorize it absolutely word for word – that's not the aim. You just need to be able to remember your key points and anecdotes. It might feel awful to you, as the speaker, if you forget a small part but remember that your audience has no idea what you planned to say. They won't notice if a small part is worded differently or missed out, as long as the rest of what you say flow well enough.

If you're brave enough, once you have the words memorized well enough to feel confident, try recording yourself delivering the speech or presentation. This can feel a bit embarrassing, especially if you're already nervous, but it's worth the effort. Watching it back will help you spot any nervous behaviors that you might not have been aware of. You can also check that your body language is congruous with your words and your tone.

Managing Nerves

No matter how well-prepared you are, you may still experience nerves. One of the most well-known pieces of advice is to imagine your audience naked. This could work, but there are lots of other less distracting ways to calm your nerves!

Before you begin speaking, ideally somewhere private, adopt a power pose for a minute or two. This is an open stance, feet wider than hip width, shoulders back, hands on hips, and chest puffed out. Tilt your chin slightly upwards. Holding this kind of power pose for a minute or two has been proven to boost confidence by increasing testosterone and lowering the stress hormone cortisol. If you can, keep a glass of water on hand in case your mouth goes dry. Take a small sip before you start and then as and when you need it – within reason. This is a great tip, but make sure that sipping the water doesn't become a nervous tic of its own that distracts the audience.

Concentrate on your breathing and speaking slowly. Don't worry that you'll sound silly. Most of us speak faster than we realize, and this betrays our nerves. Speaking slowly will stop your mind racing ahead and help your audience take your words in.

Audience Attention Span

One of the things that concern most people about public speaking is that all the attention will be on them. In reality, the hardest thing about public speaking is getting and keeping the audience's attention.

The average person can only concentrate on a speaker for around twenty minutes before their mind wanders. This is even shorter if they aren't engaged with what you're saying. And if there are external distractions happening, then you've got an even bigger battle on your hands.

Things like the temperature of the room, noise from outside the room, other audience members talking among themselves, or televisions in the background are all common distractions. There are several ways to deal with these distractions. Ideally, avoid them or remove them. If you can't remove the distractions – for example, a loud conference happening in an adjacent room, then try and overcome the issue.

Perhaps try turning up the volume on your microphone, and ensuring all the doors are closed. Failing that, call attention to the distraction and then make light of it. For example "It sounds like they're having a great time in the other room. Let's see if I can entertain you just as much!" By doing this, people will recognize the distraction and make a more conscious effort to ignore it while you speak.

Reading Your Audience and Adapting
As you deliver your speech or presentation, you may begin to get a sense of how your audience is receiving the material. The chances are that you've pre-prepared and practiced what you're going to say. So, if you pick up on signals that it's not been well received by your audience, it can be devastating. If this happens, don't let it completely

derail you. Instead, remember that they may be unconsciously reacting to your body language rather than the content of your presentation. The first thing to do is quickly assess your tone and body language to make sure you're hitting the right note.

If your body language and tone are good, but you still seem to be losing your audience don't be afraid to pause at an appropriate point and invite questions. This will give you the opportunity to address anything that you may have said that cause your audience to disagree or become disengaged. If you can address those things quickly, you can regain their interest and continue with the rest of your speech or presentation.

Case Study of Public Speaking

Jessica had avoided public speaking for most of her life. Other than a couple of stilted and awkward class presentations in college, there had been no need to speak in front of an audience. After leaving college, she started work for a software provider in their sales administration department. She worked hard and achieved promotion after only a year. However, her new role as a customer success manager meant that she'd have to give regular presentations to new and existing clients.

Jessica was terrified. Not only would she have to speak in front of an audience, but she'd have to do it regularly as a key part of her new role. She knew she needed to overcome her fear of public speaking fast. She started by preparing a template presentation, which she practiced delivering while regarding herself. As excruciating as it was watching her presentations back, Jessica was then able to pinpoint any issues with her body language. She also gained insight into her speed of speaking, tone of voice and general pinch points in the presentation that could be improved.

By choosing one issue to rectify one issue at a time, Jessica was able to break it down into easy and manageable steps. She started with addressing her body language, knowing that displaying more confident body language would trick her own brain into making her feel more confident. Once her body language during the presentations was right, Jessica noticed that the speed of speaking had also naturally slowed down. She then moved on to memorizing her key points in the presentation and making sure that her presentation slides were not overloaded.

Once Jessica was happy with her presentation recordings, she enlisted a group of close friends to deliver a practice presentation. This allowed her to practice delivering to an audience before getting in front of actual clients. The friends were impressed but had some additional feedback for her to tweak.

When Jessica needed to deliver a presentation to her actual clients, she was much calmer and more collected. She still experienced some nerves before speaking, but her thorough preparation meant that these didn't have a big impact on her and her clients provided great feedback at the end.

Public speaking is largely about confidence, and confidence is often all about your personal mindset. When you believe in yourself and what you're saying, that shines through and makes you appear more confident and more genuine to others.

In the next chapter, we'll look at how your personality and

your mindset have an impact on your communication skills, and how to use this to your advantage.

Chapter 8 – Personality and Mindset

"There is an amazing power getting to know your inner self and learning how to use it and not fight with the world. If you know what makes you happy, your personality, interests, and capabilities, just use them, and everything else flows beautifully."
Juhi Chawla

Personality

Your personality is a combination of your behavior, characteristics, attitude, and style. These combine to give you your own unique way of perceiving things and seeing the world. Many factors influence your personality including your past experiences, family background, current environment, and education.

What's Your Personality?
Knowing your personality type allows you to understand how other people may perceive you. To get the most out of this, you need to be honest about your personality. Answer the questions based on how you most often behave or react and try to be as objective as possible. There are no right or wrong answers.

In a similar manner to communication styles, understanding how personality affects communication can make you a better communicator with others. If you can identify other's personality traits, you'll be able to adjust your own communication style to suit their preferences better. This will increase the chances that they will listen to and understand the message you are trying to convey.

For example, someone who has a quiet and shy personality

is likely to be overwhelmed if you communicate with them in a loud, brash manner. Conversely, someone bold and loud is unlikely to listen to a meek, quiet communicator. Most personality styles respond well to an assertive style of communication, but by understanding them better, you can make small adjustments that make communication even easier.

Likable Traits
Some people are naturally more likable, more charismatic, more assertive or all three. These people have a natural advantage when it comes to communicating because people want to listen to them.

If you don't have a natural advantage, or you want to develop what you do have even further, then it's not very difficult to do. We'll cover this in more detail later in this chapter, but having a growth mindset is very helpful for assertive communication.

When you have a growth mindset, you know that you can develop any skill and that wherever you are now in terms of personality and communication skills, you can improve. People with a fixed mindset believe that who they are is set in stone. They believe that they can't change anything about their personality and that 'bad' communicators lack a natural talent that's not possible to develop.

The very fact that you picked up this book indicates that you believe on some level that you can make the changes needed to make you a better communicator.

Here are some of the most likable personality traits. These are the traits that are most likely to encourage people to warm to you.

- Actively listening.
- Good eye contact.
- Treating everyone with respect.
- Not making assumptions.
- Frequently smiling.
- Making a point of remembering people's names and small details.
- Being helpful.
- Being able to admit to mistakes and apologize.
- Being open-minded and not judgmental.
- Being positive.
- Accepting and delivering compliments in a genuine way.

This is by no means an exhaustive list. However, if you can tick most of these off as traits that you have, then you're well on the way to being likable. Don't worry if you don't meet all of these, we'll take a look in a moment at how to develop these traits.

It's also worth noting that displaying the opposite traits to these will make you more unlikeable. If you want people to listen to you and hear your message, getting them to like you is half the battle.

How to Develop More Likable Traits

Most of the traits that make you likable are all about making other people feel good about themselves. If you go into any conversation with the aim of making people feel good about themselves, you'll definitely have an advantage.

Making people feel good about themselves isn't about giving false compliments or avoiding difficult conversations, either. Let's break down how to develop each of the likable traits we identified earlier.

Actively Listening – We've covered active listening quite extensively in chapter four. As a brief summary, active listening is when you put distractions to one side and focus only on the person speaking and what they are saying. You just listen, without adding your own viewpoint or applying judgment.
If you choose only one thing from the list to implement, make it this one. It will have a profound effect on your communication skills.

Good Eye Contact – is covered in chapter six. To recap, eye contact is one of the best ways to appear assertive and confident. Making eye contact can make you come across as more genuine and likable as long as you don't hold eye contact for too long. If you normally look down, or away rather than looking directly at people when you speak to them, then make an effort to hold eye contact. Hold it for a couple of seconds before looking away and repeat this as often as you can.

Respect Others – Treating everyone with respect will make you instantly more likable, but it can be challenging to master when dealing with people who are the opposite of your personality type. Respecting others means listening to their opinions, acknowledging their ideas, and giving their opinions consideration. To show you respect others when communicating, you don't speak over them or instantly jump to provide counter-arguments. Instead, you seek to understand their point of view before providing your own. Much of this is part of active listening too.

Not Making Assumptions – Likable people ask questions rather than assume they already know the details. Making assumptions is part of how our brains are wired, so it can take some practice to really notice when we're doing this. Our brains tend to look for patterns and apply assumptive knowledge based on your own experiences. For example, you might make an assumption that if you are invited to a dinner party, the host will provide food. That's a very reasonable assumption to make, and you'd normally be correct in your assumption.

Unfortunately, we often apply assumptions incorrectly because we don't question properly. You might assume, for example, that your friend won't mind if you don't go to her birthday party. However, if you asked her the question your assumption could be incorrect. Not making assumptions, especially about other people, can dramatically boost your communication skills. The best way to stop assuming is to ask a lot of relevant questions. For example, if you're invited to a dinner party – ask if you should bring anything. When you want to skip out on your friend's party – ask them if they will be upset.

Ask Genuine Questions – When you ask relevant and genuine questions to understand another person, they feel that they are being properly considered and listened to. It helps take down barriers and prevents unfortunate misunderstandings.

Frequently Smiling – We also discussed this in the chapter on body language. Smiling will instantly make people like you more. It makes you appear open and approachable and even boosts your own mood. When you smile a lot, people naturally will find you more likable. Make it a habit to smile at people as you pass them, or when you greet them.

Making A Point Of Remembering People's Names And Small Details – Most people are somewhat self-centered.

We have so much going on in our own lives that we don't pay a lot of attention to other people. People who do remember the small details stand out. These are details like the names of people's partners, the details of their colleagues holiday, basically anything that shows that you are interested in them and have paid attention.

Think of the last time you felt irritated or annoyed because you had to repeat the same information to somebody for the second, third or fourth time. Chances are, they weren't deliberately not listening, they were probably just preoccupied with something else in the back of their mind. Now think about how delighted you were when somebody remembered something about you. Making little rhymes can help you remember details, or even keeping a small notebook.

Being Helpful – Offering to help people makes you instantly more likable. This one is easy to do if you pay attention to what people are saying. For example, if your partner is complaining that they are stressed, ask them what you can do to ease their burdens. If a colleague is swamped with work and you have enough time, ask if there's a task they could delegate to you. Of course, it's possible to be too helpful and you don't need to martyr yourself for the sake of being liked. Don't fall into the trap of expecting them to reciprocate, either. Only offer to help when you genuinely can and you don't expect anything in return.

If you really don't have the time to offer help, just empathize with them instead. But by helping people when you can, you'll immediately be more likable and improve your chances of getting a helping hand when you need it too.

Being Able To Admit To Mistakes And Apologize – This

one can be tough for people to do. We're often conditioned to see a mistake as a failure and feel embarrassed. At worst we might try to lie or hide the mistake, brush it off as someone else's fault. Yet usually, the people we respect and like the most aren't perfect. In fact, they make as many mistakes as anyone else.

The difference is that they openly accept their mistakes, apologize if needed and put it right if possible. It's a scary thing to do – at first, but once you adopt this as your personal mantra, it's actually very empowering.

<u>Being Open-Minded and Not Judgmental</u> – This is closely linked with active listening, but being non-judgmental makes people feel that they can be open and honest with you. Not only does this make you more likable, but it also increases the chances of people sharing their true thoughts and feelings with you – reducing your need to try and 'read between the lines.'

<u>Being Positive</u> – Being around negative people brings you down and being around positive people lifts you up. Everybody prefers to be around people with more positive energy about them because they make you feel good. This doesn't mean you have to be naïve, or over-the-top. But make a point of staying away from negativity. Especially negativity about other people.

Obviously, life isn't all sunshine and roses and there will be times that what you have to say about somebody or something won't be positive. You don't need to lie if someone asks what you think but stay away from mindless gossip or simply dumping your negative opinions in the mix when it isn't necessary. When you can't be completely positive, aim for constructive rather than critical and encouraging rather than disparaging.

Accepting and Delivering Compliments In A Genuine Way – Everyone loves to be complimented, but not everybody is good at accepting and receiving compliments. When giving compliments, give them freely but make them genuine. Complimenting people simply for the sake of it makes you appear false rather than likable. Luckily this one is easy to implement. If you think something positive about somebody, say it! Compliments aren't limited to people's appearance either. Compliment the way they handled themselves in a meeting or their positive qualities as a friend.

Accept Compliments Graciously – You don't have to brush them off or feel obliged to offer a compliment in return. Just a smile and a thank-you are enough.

Why Mindset Matters in Communication

There's more to your personality than your outward traits. Your mindset is also a big part of who you are, and how people perceive you. One thing that is crucial to effective communication, in particular, is having a growth mindset.

The term *'growth mindset'* was first used by psychology professor Carole Dweck. In her book, *'Mindset'*, she posited that people have either a fixed mindset or a growth mindset.

People who have a fixed mindset believe that their intelligence, character, and abilities don't change, and they can't develop new ones. For these people, failure is proof that they are naturally unable to achieve something.

People who have a growth mindset understand that their intelligence, character, and abilities can be changed. They are always learning, and that believe they can learn and develop new skills and qualities throughout their whole lives. For these people, failure is merely a learning opportunity they can grow from, and it is not evidence of their incapability to do something.

Having a fixed mindset can prevent you from reaching success in all areas of your life, not just your communication skills. In contrast, a growth mindset allows you to see past the primitive concepts of success and failure and create success in almost anything. In *'Mindset'*, Dweck comments that for people with a growth mindset, the journey is as important as the destination.

How A Growth Mindset Benefits Communication
People with a growth mindset are naturally charismatic and inspiring because they live and breathe the idea of continuous learning and improvement. When they speak, people tend to listen.

A growth mindset allows you to be a more effective communicator because you understand that every failure is an opportunity for improvement. If you experience a misunderstanding through poor communication, you don't let that define every other conversation you have. That resilience gives you the strength to keep on trying, keep on improving and therefore eventually master communication skills.

People with an affixed mindset may learn the theory of communications, but at their first failure, they would deduce that they are not good communicators and resign themselves to that label.
When you approach things with a growth mindset, you are

applying a philosophy of persistence and perseverance that numerous studies show is consistent with success. This goes for communication skills and anything else you want to achieve.

Developing A Growth Mindset

So we know that a growth mindset is a key to communication and overall success, but what if you have a fixed mindset? How can you change that?

Here are some simple ways to develop a growth mindset.

Enjoy The Process And Recognize Progress – People with a growth mindset value the process of learning just as much as they enjoy achieving a successful outcome. Don't get too hung up on getting your communication skills perfect. Take pleasure in the activity of learning excellent communication skills and enjoy the process of developing them.

Learn From Your Mistakes – While you should enjoy the learning journey and not get hung up on perfection, there's a big difference between a growth mindset and not really caring. While people with a growth mindset don't worry about failing, they do use those failures to learn and avoid making the same mistakes again. This ability to see failure as a powerful learning tool is essential to a growth mindset. Accountability is important, but an unhealthy fear of failure stifles your creativity and breeds a fixed mindset.

Be Tenacious – The old saying: if at first, you don't succeed… is a crucial part of the growth mindset. It doesn't matter how many attempts it takes. If it's an outcome worth achieving, then you should put in the effort required to learn and grow enough to achieve it. Remember that every failure is a chance to improve and brings you one step closer to success.

Seek Out Feedback – Become self-aware about where your communication strengths and weaknesses are, and how others see you. People with a growth mindset welcome feedback. They actively seek it out and take steps to improve based on the feedback of others.

How You Project Your Beliefs in What You Say

Fixed and growth mindsets are a simple way of looking at the mindset equation, but mindset covers much more than this. Your mindset is your internalization of certain beliefs. Some of these beliefs may be self-limiting, and those are the beliefs that are stopping you succeeding.

Getting rid of your self-limiting beliefs brings you one step closer to success in communication and anything else you want to achieve. Mindset is vital to communication because even if you don't realize it, the way you communicate broadcasts messages to others about your mindset that they can pick up on.

For example, someone with a self-limiting belief that they are naturally unlucky might choose not to enter a free prize draw, saying 'it's pointless, I never win anything.' Whereas someone without that limiting belief might say *'why not enter, it's free and I have as much chance of winning as anybody else.'*

This is quite a tame example, but people are often carrying around much more insidious limiting beliefs. Someone who didn't do very well at high school math because the teaching methods didn't suit them might believe that they are doomed to a poor level of numeracy forever. Instead of addressing the issue and finding a way to learn and develop the relevant math skills they might instead just avoid any activities or opportunities that require math skills.

Unaddressed, limiting beliefs can become something of a vicious cycle. Your words are constantly reaffirming your own self-limiting beliefs. They're potentially also reinforcing that view with the people you speak to. Take the example of the person who believes they are 'bad at math.' When offered a promotion at work, for example, that involves report-writing and data, they might tell their boss that they can't do that. They may say it's because they're 'bad at math.' Their boss may accept this to be true and make a mental note to not look to this person for promotion, or anything where they may need to be good with numbers.

If that person had a different mindset, they might resolve to find a way to learn math and perhaps even gain a qualification. They may not become a math prodigy or discover an untapped natural talent for algebra. However, with the right mindset and a little determination, developing the practical math skills that they would need for a promotion is unlikely to be out of their reach.

One way to change your mindset is to change your words. That's one of the reasons that affirmations are so popular. It's not a magical incantation, but it works because you are sending your brain a message by feeding it more positive words. Over time this can rewire how you perceive yourself.

In the same way that what you think about yourself impacts how you behave; other people will have beliefs and opinions about you. These beliefs are partly based on a combination of your body language, and the way you speak. For example, saying mostly positive things will mean that people view you in a more positive light. If you are constantly telling people how useless you are, they will begin to believe it at least on some level too.

Make a habit of noticing what you say to and about yourself. When your words about yourself are negative, try and replace them in your mind with something positive. For example, instead of saying *'I'm not a good communicator,'* say *'I'm studying communication skills so I can become a better communicator.'* Or *'my communication skills are improving all the time.'*

Make a commitment to yourself to develop your mindset. Having the right mindset can make you more resilient, more successful, and more approachable. All of these things will make you a better communicator in general, but in particular, they will help you with one of the trickiest aspects of good communication: managing conflict.

Conflict is something most of us seek to avoid, but having the skills to handle it properly can be life-changing. In the next chapter, we'll look at what causes conflict, and how to handle it without damaging relationships.

Chapter 9 – Managing Conflict Thru Better Communication

Conflict

It's something that most of us prefer to avoid, but unfortunately, it is sometimes unavoidable. A conflict arises when your own needs or goals and the needs or goals of another person are at odds. At first glance it seems that only one of you can have what they want or need.

Conflict can be common in the workplace when people are competing to claim a piece of the department budget. Money is a common source of conflict in relationships too. When there is a finite amount of money that can be spent, it's not always possible for everyone to get what they want. Conflict isn't restricted to money issues, however.

Most of us will experience some level of conflict every day. A lot of the literature around managing conflict is aimed at managers for use in the workplace, but conflict can arise anywhere, not just at work.

At home, there might be a conflict between roommates or partners who both work full-time about how chores should be shared. Teenagers and their parents may experience conflict over how much autonomy the teenager has, cellphone usage, and curfew times to name a few. Anybody who has experienced bringing up children can tell you that the most intense, frustrating and nonsensical conflicts you'll ever experience are with a stubborn toddler.

Conflict is a natural, if not always a pleasant part of communicating with other people. Developing your skills in conflict management can help you reduce the stress of handling conflict, and even sometimes head off conflict before it occurs.

It's important to recognize that conflict isn't always a bad thing. Conflict is only a situation where the goals or needs of two or more people don't match, and it isn't always a bad thing. In fact, some of the most productive discussions can come out of initial conflict. When you understand how to handle conflict effectively, you can develop richer and more rewarding relationships both at work and at home.

Why Do We Often Try To Avoid Dealing With Conflict?

Conflict can take quite an emotional toll on people, which is one of the reasons many people choose to avoid it where possible. Conflict happens when we perceive a threat to our well-being. That threat can be physical or emotional, and it can be as simple as just not getting what we want. Our primitive lizard brain, the amygdala, kicks into action and prompts the fight-or-flight response, our typical reaction to any perceived threat.

When that happens, your body is flooded with the stress hormone cortisol. Because of this, conflict can create the same effects in you as stress and anxiety: rapid heartbeat, perspiration, stomach cramps, headaches, muscle tension and even panic attacks.

If the conflict is drawn-out or ongoing, the psychological and physiological effects can be quite severe. The longer conflict drags on, the more afraid we tend to become of addressing the situation. We might hope the problem will solve itself. Or, we might quietly simmer with anger and frustration because we assume the other person won't be willing to listen or negotiate.

In many cases, if the conflict is with somebody that we perceive as more powerful, it can seem hopeless to try to resolve it. Whether your conflict is with your boss, or your mother-in-law, if your past experience has been that they always 'win', addressing the issue can seem pointless. Unfortunately, when you don't address conflict, it just carries on in the background. Eventually you become more frustrated and angry, perhaps eventually having an emotional outburst at something that seems trivial – further undermining your position in the conflict.

Addressing conflict assertively is a brave move for most people. You need to have the courage to speak up and voice your opinions. You also need to have the emotional maturity and resilience to listen to the other person's point of view and apply empathy and an open mind to their concerns. You may need to acknowledge your own mistakes. All of this can be uncomfortable to do, but the benefits are worth it.

Taking an assertive approach to conflict management not only allows you to stop letting conflict simmer in the background, it also earns you respect among your colleagues, friends, and loved ones.

Identifying Potential Conflict
There are often early warning signs that conflict is brewing. If you can recognize these signs, it gives you the chance to prepare how to handle any impending conflict or even stop it in its tracks.

Some of the warning signs of conflict can be:

Defensive Or Aggressive Body Language – As we discussed in chapter six, even when people guard their words carefully, there are usually signals via body language that give a little insight into how they really feel. Folded arms, clenched jaw, and a chin tilted downward are all signs that someone isn't taking something well.

Increased Absence At Work – It's natural to try to avoid stressful situations and conflict, so people may begin to take more time off work than they would usually, to avoid the problem. It's rarely an effective strategy, but it's incredibly common.

Avoiding Spending Time Together In Personal Relationships – In the same way that people might skip work to avoid a conflict situation, in a personal relationship they may try to avoid spending time with the other person. If someone suddenly becomes too busy to spend time with you and this is out of character, it could be a sign that conflict is brewing.

Changes In Behavior – When a normally talkative person becomes quiet and withdrawn, or someone who is normally mild-mannered becomes irritable and short-tempered, it could be a sign of conflict. Of course, this can also happen when a person is under general stress rather than specifically related to potential conflict.

Emotive or Sarcastic Language – If a person is suddenly using a lot more emotive language than usual, or is making uncharacteristic sarcastic comments, it could indicate an issue. It's especially common in people with passive-aggressive tendencies to become more generally difficult instead of addressing the conflict directly.

When you spot these signs in others, the best way to deal with it is to discuss what's happening. Don't make assumptions regarding why the other person may feel that there is a conflict. Instead, ask them open questions in a non-threatening way to get to the bottom of what's causing the issue.

In many cases, there's a simple misunderstanding that can be cleared up immediately before it escalates into a conflict. If, however, there's a genuine conflict situation, you'll need to employ conflict management techniques to sort it out.

Conflict Management Styles

The first step to managing conflict with others is to understand how you and others personally handle conflict. There are various styles of handling conflict, and most of us have a specific preference ranging on a scale from aggressive to cooperative.

People with a highly aggressive conflict style aim to satisfy only their own concerns during any conflict situation. People with a highly cooperative conflict style aim to satisfy the other party's concerns during any conflict situation.

Several conflict styles lie in between these two extremes:

Competitive
This is the most aggressive conflict style. It's a very power-oriented style where the person using it will put their own needs above everything and everybody else. They do this using whatever tools or authority are at their disposal.

Competitive conflict management isn't always a bad thing, and there are times when it may be necessary to use this style. However, in most situations, it's too heavy-handed and can seriously damage relationships. It can also mean that you overlook a potential win-win situation where nobody must come out of the conflict as the loser.

Collaborating

The collaborative style is something of a middle ground. A person using this style tries to find common ground and come up with a solution that keeps both parties happy.

The right solution will make sure that everybody's concerns are considered. Although there may have to be an element of compromise, nobody should have to concede something very important to them.

A collaborative style can strengthen relationships and tends to create innovative solutions. Unfortunately, the 'perfect' solution doesn't always exist, and even when it does the collaborative style takes a lot of time. If the other person or people are too resistant, it may be impossible to take a collaborative approach.

Compromising

A compromising style is very similar to a collaborative style. The difference is that someone using a compromising style will sacrifice of some theirs or the other party's concerns while still trying to satisfy both as much as possible.

This is a faster way to resolve an issue than collaborating, but will obviously involve some compromise – often from both parties. It's a good choice for preserving relationships.

Complying

This style is the most cooperative, at the detriment of the person using it. It's the opposite of the competitive style. A person using a compliant style will look to satisfy the needs of the other person over satisfying their own.

This style can be excellent for building or preserving relationships. It's often the best option when you don't have very strong feelings about the outcome of a disagreement but the other person does. Adopting this style too often, however, can lead to you being a *'pushover'* and people may attempt to take advantage.

Avoiding
Avoidance is completely unaggressive and completely uncooperative. A person using this style simply ignores or walks away from the conflict.

It can be a good style to adopt if the situation is particularly emotional and you need time to cool down. If you use it inappropriately, it can cause resentment towards you, and mean that nothing is ever resolved.

It's often best used as a short-term style when you need a little space to cool off and intend to return to the discussion and resolve it later. In these cases, being upfront and clear with the other person that you just need a little space to think is advisable.

Which Is The Best Conflict Management Style?

There's no one right style to use all the time, although each different conflict situation will have one most appropriate style to use. Even avoidance and aggression have their place in appropriate conflict management, but these situations should be rare. Being able to identify and employ the right style at the right time is essential for smooth conflict management.

Most people have preferred styles that come naturally to them, but you can switch between the styles depending on the situation. It's not uncommon to rely exclusively on one style, and this is when you will probably run into problems managing conflict when the style doesn't fit the situation.

However, there's more to managing conflict than choosing the correct style for the situation. In order to choose the correct style, you need to have a good understanding of the situation. The first step to this is to understand the perceived threat on both sides, and this is where an assertive communication style is crucial for heading off conflict.

It's also important to take the environment into consideration. Remember that conflict is stressful, for all involved, so try to choose a place to discuss any issues that is calm and relaxed, with a good temperature. The space should be private enough to not be overheard, yet large enough to not feel confining.

Before initiating any discussion, identify what the perceived threat to your own well-being is. This can be harder than it seems, because often there are underlying fears that we don't immediately recognize. Then, you need to try to understand exactly what the other person is perceiving as a threat. This is even more difficult, as the other person will be applying their own perceptions and filters that you may not be aware of.

Once you believe you understand exactly what is at stake for both parties, you'll need to be ready to address that, along with the emotional aspects of the conflict. Conflicts are often highly emotional, but these emotions are normally driven by five core concerns, identified by Roger Fisher and Daniel Shapiro in *'Beyond Reason: Using Emotions as you Negotiate'*. Understanding these can help you navigate the tricky waters of negotiation.

The Five Core Human Concerns

The five core concerns represent the basic human desires that drive our emotions in any conflict. By focusing on these core concerns, you can effectively reduce the length of a conflict and ensure that any negotiation or discussion goes as smoothly as possible.

These core concerns are:

- Appreciation,
- Affiliation,
- Autonomy,
- Status,
- and Role.

Appreciation
Demonstrating appreciation involves understanding and valuing the other person's point of view. Applying appreciation quickly can head off any impending trouble before it begins. Even if a conflict does arise, keeping this core concern at the forefront can help resolve the conflict quickly without damaging relationships.

To demonstrate appreciation, you should acknowledge that you can see the value of the other person's words, actions, or emotions.

For example, in a conflict about whether a couple should

save money or splurge on a vacation, demonstrating appreciation means listening to the other person's point of view. Once they have had their say, you might respond with something like, *"I know we've both worked hard this year, and that's meant long hours in the office. I can see why you think a vacation would be good for us, given that we've not spent as much quality time together recently as we'd like."*

Demonstrating that you understand and value their feelings about the situation, before you go ahead and present your own feelings, helps to reduce the tension. It also demonstrates that they are being taken seriously. This will make them much more open and less defensive when you present your own thoughts and feelings.

Affiliation

Applying affiliation involves encouraging a collaborative approach. This detracts from the *'me'* vs *'you'* conflict dynamic and tries to turn the situation into a team effort to solve a problem- making it an 'us' dynamic.

To apply affiliation, you'll need to find some common ground. Look for what you do have in common, or try to use small talk to reinforce some common interests. The more related to the conflict, the better, but any common ground is good. Shared sporting interests, television shows, mutual friends. Anything that demonstrates the ways you are similar will help to build an affiliation.

Pay attention to the language you use. Pronouns like 'I' and 'you' should be switched for 'we' and 'us' wherever possible. The aim is always to build and maintain a picture of both parties working collaboratively, and not separately.

Autonomy

Autonomy relates to people's desire to feel that they have some control. A lot of conflicts occur because people feel they have been overlooked in decisions or actions that have impacted them.

For example, your neighbor may become upset if you build a house extension that blocks some of their sunlight. While the loss of sunlight appears to be the issue, often it's the fact that they feel overlooked and unheard that is causing the real hostility.

Autonomy concerns are frequently at the root of parent-child conflict. Children want to feel autonomous from a young age, and parents want to protect their children from any bad or dangerous decisions they may make. This can lead to frequent power struggles where the child tries to assert themselves and the parent thwarts those attempts.

Sometimes, these can be averted by giving the child choices. For example, if your toddler demands chocolate for breakfast and has a tantrum when they don't get it, try offering them a choice of breakfasts instead. By saying *'do you want pancakes, or toast?'* you're giving them a sense of control and autonomy while limiting the options to choices that you are also comfortable with.

With adults, autonomy can be addressed by consulting others before taking any actions that might impact them. Unfortunately, this isn't always as easy as it sounds because you may not realize that they are impacted by your actions or decisions until it's too late. Thinking through carefully who might be affected when you're making any large decisions is always a good habit to build.

Status
Status is about people's need to be recognized for their

strengths and achievements. When people feel that their sense of status is being challenged, they can become very defensive or aggressive. If a person believes they are superior in some aspect to the other person, they may attempt to leverage this during a disagreement.

For example, a partner who earns substantially more money may feel that they have more status in a discussion about household finances than the other partner.

Leveraging your status in a conflict can work in terms of ensuring you 'win' the current argument. Used incorrectly, however, it can lead to the other person becoming very resentful and can damage relationships. You can apply the status concern in a positive way during negotiations by deferring to the other person's expertise or asking their advice. This demonstrates that you have respect for their status and can also demonstrate that you aren't misusing your own status in order to achieve your own goals.

Role
Role is about the specific role people play in the conflict, and that role can change over the course of the disagreement. All too often, both people take on the role of competitor, and nobody is taking on the role of listener, mediator, problem-solver or advocate.

You can't control the role the other person plays, so to effectively address this concern, you need to identify what role the other person is playing. Then, choose your own role to complement that. The roles you both play can change numerous times during the discussion. For example, while the other person is listing their concerns, you may want to adopt the role of listener, demonstrating that you are listening and understanding their viewpoints. When they finish, you can take on the role of problem-solver to try to address the issues, or it may be more appropriate to take up an advocate role.

Having an awareness of the different roles and choosing you role wisely can help to smooth over conflict and aid negotiations.

Real Life Case Study – Managing Conflict Positively

Maria's husband Brent was offered a great promotion at work. It was a lot more money, but it also involved moving to a new state and uprooting their family.

Brent and Maria both had different views on whether Brent should take the promotion, given the impact on Maria's job and social life. She was especially concerned about the potential disruption to their thirteen-year-old son's schooling. Their disagreement was causing conflict between them and putting a strain on their marriage. To make the situation worse, their son Bradley had his own views which didn't match either Brent's or Maria's.

Brent wanted to take the promotion because he felt it would provide a better quality of life for the family longer-term. Maria didn't want to uproot the whole family at such a crucial time in Bradley's life. She wanted Brent to have the opportunity, and she would enjoy the benefits of the pay increase, but she wanted to keep Bradley in the same school. She also didn't want to leave her own job which she enjoyed. She was, however, willing to concede that Brent's income would offset the loss of her own in the short-term while she looked for another job.

Bradley felt that the promotion would be good for his father and the family overall, but he didn't want to move schools and leave his friends. His opinion was that Brent and Maria should move and sell the house and leave Bradley to live with his maternal grandparents during term time. Neither Brent nor Maria agreed with Bradley's solution, and both of them wanted the family to remain living together under the same roof.

Each time Maria tried to tackle the subject the conflict would seem overwhelming. Any discussion would inevitably end with somebody getting up and walking out before a solution or decision could be reached. Brent was becoming more and more stressed as time was running out to accept or decline the promotion, and they still hadn't reached a definite agreement. The atmosphere in the house as a result of the conflict was uncomfortable for everybody, and they'd begun avoiding each other as much as possible.

Eventually, Maria decided that enough was enough, and she decided to brush up on her conflict management skills to try to reach a resolution to the issue. Maria could see that Bradley's autonomy was being threatened, and that both Brent and Maria had dismissed his concerns, meaning that he didn't feel appreciated. For Brent, his status as head of the family was being challenged because Maria and Bradley didn't agree with his view of the situation. Maria also felt that her own views weren't being appreciated.

Bradley's style was mostly competitive, despite his insistence that his solution was the perfect compromise. Brent switched between competitive and compromising modes, and Maria's main style up until now had been mostly compromising. This mix of styles hadn't helped them resolve the issue. Even though Brent and Maria were sometimes both in compromise mode, they all felt too strongly about the outcome for anyone to concede enough ground.

Armed with this new knowledge, Maria was determined to resolve the conflict. Because they all had such strong feelings, and the stakes were high, she felt that a collaborative approach was the best option for such a big decision. It might take some time, but between them they could find a solution that left everyone feeling satisfied.

Maria began by calling a family meeting, and immediately acknowledging Bradley's concerns. She explained that she could see the merit in his proposal, and how it would solve some of the problem. However, him staying with his grandparents wasn't an option, as it was too much pressure for his grandparents as well as not being what his parents wanted. She also acknowledged that he should have a say in what happened and that the solution needed to address everybody's main concerns.

Next, she acknowledged Brent's status as the main earner in their household. She also acknowledged that it was important that he was able to continue to develop his career with the support of his family. Then, she clearly laid out her own concerns about being able to continue her own career and to see Bradley remain in the same school.

The discussion was calmer than any they had experienced so far, because Maria was able to address the emotional concerns that everyone had. But they still hadn't found a solution. Maria concentrated on building a sense of affiliation, reminding them that they were a family, and that they should work together to find a solution. She was careful to use 'we' and 'us' as much as possible, to foster a sense of inclusion.

After the meeting, they hadn't reached a solution, but everyone was feeling more optimistic that there might be a way to meet everybody's needs. The atmosphere became more relaxed, and they were able to enjoy a little family time together.

The next day, Brent came home with some news for the family. He had approached his current boss about the predicament. After a conference call with the department head in the other office, they had agreed that Brent could work remotely for 80% of the time. This meant spending just one week a month in the new office.

This solution would mean that some of Brent's salary increase would need to be used on accommodation in another state for five days per month. However, there would still be enough left to significantly improve the family finances. It also meant that Maria and Bradley wouldn't have to move. The family all agreed that this was the best possible outcome in the situation.

Managing conflict is an essential skill and, as you can see, adopting an assertive communication style puts you in the right frame of mind to handle conflict positively and find a solution. There's a lot of overlap between good conflict management and assertive communication: active listening, acknowledging views and opinions of others, remaining calm, stating your position without resorting to blame.

In the next chapter, we'll recap some key learning points and look at how to put it all into practice in order to become a more assertive communicator.

Chapter 10 – Putting It All Into Practice

"To be passive is to let others decide for you. To be aggressive is to decide for others. To be assertive is to decide for yourself. And to trust that there is enough, that you are enough."
Edith Eva Eger

Assertive Communication Techniques

We've covered various aspects of assertive communication throughout this book, and in this chapter, we'll be looking at some very specific assertiveness techniques that you can implement. These are all specific examples of behaviors that assertive people demonstrate, and that can be easily applied to common situations.

Saying No
A key part of being assertive is making sure your own needs are met and your opinions are heard, without resorting to aggression. A common one that a lot of people struggle with is just saying no.

Assertive people are comfortable saying *'no.'* They understand that they don't have to provide a reason, but will often provide a sound and logical reason if they do have one. The next time somebody asks you to do something that you don't want to do, try responding politely with a *'no.'*

For example, if you're asked to take on extra work, but you're already swamped, you can simply say *'I'd love to be able to help, but I've got more than enough work already.'*

Ask For More Time

It's impossible to always have the information and answers you might need to hand. An assertive communicator recognizes that this is normal and simply asks for any additional time they might need.

This can be applied whether you need time to consider your feelings about a situation, or you need to research tangible facts before answering a question.

For this technique to be effective, you need to deliver your request for more time confidently and calmly. Simply state what you need the time for, and how long it will take. For example, *'I'll need to check on the facts for you, how about we reconvene tomorrow?'* Or, *'I'm not sure how I feel about that. I'd like to take some time to consider it, let's discuss it again next week.'*

Using 'I' Statements

This technique is best used when you want to address somebody else's behavior. Criticizing others can cause emotions to flare and can make people become defensive and unwilling to listen. One reason for this is that we tend to use blaming language when addressing other people's actions.

Using *'I'* statements forces you to take responsibility for your own feelings and avoids placing blame on the other person. By using *'I'* statements, you can address emotive issues without immediately putting the other person into defensive mode.

For example, instead of saying *'you're late,'* you can say *'I was expecting you at two o'clock.'* Instead of saying *'you always forget to lock the door,'* you can say *'I get frustrated when you forget to lock the door.'*

Rehearse Situations or Have A 'Script'

If a scenario makes you feel anxious, rehearsing how you might behave and respond in that situation can help. For example, if you're due to have a performance review with your manager, try playing out in your mind. Consider all the different ways it could play out, and what your manager might say along with your possible responses.

For each potential question you might be asked or challenge you think your manager might give, consider how you want to respond. Develop a loose script that you can use to answer key points. The script is simply to help you organize your thoughts, you wouldn't take an actual script into the meeting. However, by considering and rehearsing some potential responses you will reduce the anxiety you might feel. It can also prevent any potentially awkward moments where you struggle to find an appropriate response.

Be A Broken Record

This technique can be used when somebody isn't taking 'no' for an answer or is refusing to accept what you are saying to them. It's a very simple concept, where you simply repeat your initial response until the other person finally accepts it.

You can reword your response slightly each time, but you need to keep the message the same. For example, if somebody asks you to attend a party that you don't want to attend, you might respond with *'I can't make it on that day.'*

If the other person doesn't accept that, challenging why you can't make it, you might simply say *'I can't make it on that day, I have a prior appointment.'* If they continue to challenge, you would just repeat that you cannot make it on that day.

The key to making this work properly is to repeat yourself without displaying any anger, irritation, frustration or anxiety. Your body language and tone should be as calm and neutral as possible. Once the other person sees that you won't change your stance, they will usually back off.

Fogging

Fogging is a technique where you accept unwarranted or malicious criticism by calmly acknowledging that there may be an element of truth to the remark, without accepting that their comment has any real merit.

It's a way to defuse a situation where someone with an aggressive style is trying to get a reaction from you. Instead of the expected reaction of refuting the criticism or becoming upset, you simply calmly respond with a mild acknowledgment that sidesteps their aggressive intent.

For example, if someone says *'Why did you take that route? That was a stupid thing to do!'* You might respond with *'Yes, I could have taken a different route and arrived quicker.'*

Negative Inquiry

Negative inquiry is another way of deflecting criticism by asking questions instead of arguing or becoming defensive.

Take the previous example of someone saying *'Why did you take that route? That was a stupid thing to do!'* If you were using negative inquiry, you might say *'Oh, I see. Which route should I have taken?'*

Again, the key is to do this is a very calm and non-confrontational manner, without sarcastic tone, so that your attempt at assertive negative inquiry isn't mistaken for passive-aggression.

Active Voice

Assertive people use the active voice more frequently than the passive voice. Active voice is when it is very clear exactly who is performing an action.

For example, *'The report must be delivered today'* is an example of passive voice, because it isn't clear who is completing the action of delivering the report. *'James must deliver the report today,'* is the active voice, because it is very clear who is expected to deliver the report. A simple test of whether something is active or passive is to add *'by zombies'* to the end of the sentence. If it still makes sense, the sentence is passive.

Consider the following sentences:

- *I was taught to stand correctly (by zombies)*
- *I learned to drive (by zombies)*
- *The report has been written already (by zombies)*
- *Jane already wrote the report (by zombies)*

A and C are passive voice, because the addition of *'by zombies'* doesn't make the sentence incorrect, whereas B and D are active voice. By choosing to use the active voice, assertive people avoid ambiguity and misunderstandings.

Set Clear Boundaries

If you struggle to set boundaries, then other people will find it easy to walk all over you. Assertive people are clear about their boundaries and they set them clearly, If their boundaries are overstepped, they reassert them quickly.

By not being afraid to stand up for themselves and challenge people who try to push their boundaries, assertive people protect their self-esteem and earn respect from others.

Address Specific Behaviors

Assertive people don't shy away from addressing issues, but when they do they focus on criticizing the behavior and not the person. By focusing on the specific behavior, they allow the other person to understand exactly what needs to change, and allow them to take on board the feedback without feeling personally attacked.

This works best when combined with *'I'* statements and delivered in a calm and non-confrontational manner.

By implementing these techniques and the other information within this book, you will begin to become a more assertive communicator. So far, we've focused specifically on verbal communication, although some of these techniques can be applied to written communication as well.

However, in our modern world we frequently communicate in writing. Emails, texts, messenger apps, social media are often daily occurrences, and they can have very different rules and etiquette than the more formal medium of letters.

In our last chapter, we'll take a look at how the different methods of written communication vary from verbal communication, and how to apply assertive communication technique to those methods.

Chapter 11 – Assertive Written Communication

"Verbal communication is much easier than written communication, because words act on the feelings in a mysterious way and easily establish a current of sympathy between people; it is for this reason that an orator is able to produce conviction by arguments which do not seem very comprehensible to any one reading the speech later."
Georges Sorel

How To Use Written Communication Assertively

Only 30 years ago, most written communication was in the form of letters that tended to have a more formal feel. Most people wouldn't write an enormous amount of letters a week, unless they were writing them as part of their job. If you wanted to speak to somebody who wasn't in the same room as you, you would pick up the telephone and call them.

With the rise of modern technology, the internet, smartphones and social media many of our daily interactions are now in writing. Verbal communication skills are still very important, but being able to get your message across in writing is just as essential – and often requires a slightly different set of skills.

The Difference Between Written and Verbal Communication

Written communication is different from verbal communication. If you were to write down, word-for-word what you would say face-to-face, it potentially wouldn't receive the same response as if you delivered the message verbally.

So why is writing so different to verbal communication?

We discussed in chapter six how we depend on body language to interpret the real meaning behind somebody's words. Yet in writing, there is no body language to give us an indication of the other person's emotional state. None of the non-verbal cues we normally rely on are present, and we only have the actual words to rely on.

In the same manner, there is no clear indication of the tone when a message is in writing. We rely on tone to tell us if someone is serious or joking, if they're angry or upset, or there's an element of their message that they want to emphasize. Tone is particularly useful on telephone calls when we don't have any body language clues. However, with writing, all you have are the words on the screen or the page – you have to make certain assumptions about the tone of the communication.

Because we don't have any of the non-verbal cues, we mostly rely on our own filters to identify the tone of the message – and that can cause misunderstandings. What might be considered an assertive face-to-face discussion can be interpreted as an aggressive email, even though the same words are used.

Just like verbal communication, there are varying degrees of formality with written communication. The differences between written and verbal communication are most noticeable in a business environment, where formality is standard. Letters that are often quite formal tend to be reserved for official or business use. Emails can be either personal or professional, and so slightly different etiquette applies depending on who you are emailing. Text messages are more commonly informal, and social media is also normally quite informal.

Yet even within these mediums there are exceptions. LinkedIn is a social media site that is designed for professionals to connect with each other. As such, posts tends to have a more formal tone, and there are frequent discussions on the platform over what people do and don't find appropriate for posting. On Facebook, a much more personal platform, posts are rarely professional in tone.

One of the big positives of written communication is that you have the luxury of choosing your words very carefully. You can revise anything before you send it and correct any mistakes you might have made.

Assertive Written Communication Tips

<u>Spelling and Grammar</u>
One big difference between spoken and written communication is that written communication needs good spelling and grammar in order to be effective in delivering the right message. This is especially true in business communications, but most written communications need good spelling and grammar in order to get the message across effectively.

Ideally, you should always review and proofread your writing before you send it. Even with personal messages and posts, bad grammar or spelling mistakes can obscure your original meaning and cause confusion. Not everyone is concerned about spelling and grammar, but many people are and making sure that your writing is grammatically correct can help you gain credibility.

Of course, the main objective of any communication is to get a message across. If you happen to make a spelling or grammar mistake that doesn't make the meaning of your message clear, it's not a disaster. Especially in personal communications. However, getting into the habit of proofreading everything can prevent some embarrassing mistakes and protect your credibility.

If you're nervous about your spelling and grammar, there are plenty of apps and software options that can help. Most email clients and word processors have a built-in spellcheck function. Smartphone keyboards often have an autocorrect feature, but they quite often make inappropriate corrections that can lead to embarrassing (and occasionally hilarious) mistakes.

Advanced options like Grammarly can pick up when you may have used the wrong word, and can make suggestions that make your writing sharper. These are optional, however. A quick proofread and a little care is normally all that is needed to avoid common mistakes.

Managing Tone in Written Communications
So, when you can't use your tone of voice and body language, how do you make sure that your message is interpreted in the right way?

Consider the Type of Medium Being Used
The first thing to consider is the medium of communication. As a general rule of thumb, text message, messaging apps and social media (with the possible exception of LinkedIn) are the least formal. Letter and email are more formal. Formal doesn't always mean 'stiff'

and a conversational tone is appropriate, especially when the email is to a colleague that you have a close working relationship with. An email to a group of directors might have a less conversational style.

Is the Tone Suited to Your Recipient?

The second thing to consider is the person receiving the message. A social media status will be potentially seen by lots of people, so consider if it's suitable for everyone on your friends list. If it's not, Facebook allows you to tailor who can and can't see your status updates. So you can post a status without your boss or your parents seeing it, if you want to do so. As a general rule of thumb, don't post anything you wouldn't be happy to have quoted back at you in the future.

For emails, texts and messages, they are usually sent to one person or a small group of people. You should consider who is receiving the communication and how they are likely to interpret the message. If you're sending a text to your boss to tell them you won't be in work because you're sick, you'll need to keep it fairly formal. Inviting a close friend out for a couple of drinks, however, needs a different tone entirely.

So, with the differences in medium aside, how do you make sure that your tone is carried across in a written communication?

Ask yourself these three questions before you write anything:

- *Who is this communication for?*
- *Am I confident that a conversational tone is appropriate or should I stick to formal?*

- *What is it that I need them to know or understand?*

Although you may write your communication with a particular tone in mind, you need to be aware that the recipient will interpret it based on several variables.

How they read it will be influenced by:

- *their existing relationship with you,*
- *their past experiences with others,*
- *and their current mood among others.*

However, there are some steps you can take to make sure that your intended tone is as clear as possible. Unless you know the person very well, make the assumption that when they read your message they will be tired, stressed and in a bad mood. Put yourself in their shoes as much as possible.

Wording
Word choice can make a big difference when you're communicating in writing. In a face-to-face conversation, the other person's body language and reactions will tell you if you need to adjust what you are saying. In writing, you won't get the opportunity to do this so it's even more important that you make good word choices upfront.

Some general rules of thumb are:

Avoid Jargon or Unnecessarily Complicated Words –
Using jargon is always best avoided. Even if the recipient is likely to understand the jargon, communications are always clearer when they are written in plain, commonly used words.

Avoid 'Filler' Words That Might Water Down The

Message – Words like *'basically,' 'honestly,' 'thought'* and *'just'* can distract from your message. So instead of writing *'I just thought I'd let you know that I'll be ten minutes late'*, you would write, *'I'll be ten minutes late.'* At their best, filler words like this don't serve much of a purpose, and at worst they can make you seem unsure or wishy-washy.

Avoid Blaming Language – which will most likely put the other person into defensive mode immediately.

Use An Active Voice Rather Than Passive – Passive sentences tend to be longer and harder to read. They can also make your message sound vague, so sticking to active voice is always the best choice.

Re-read – If you're responding to a message or email, make sure you've read the original email carefully. Apply the same rules that you would when actively listening face-to-face. Your response should ideally acknowledge any points raised and demonstrate that you have read and understood their message.

Don't Respond Immediately If You're Angry, Upset or Frustrated – The beauty of written communication is that you don't have to reply straight away. Take some time to cool off and let your emotions settle before typing a response. If you absolutely need to type a response straight away, type it and then take five minutes to calm down before reading it back and making any necessary changes.

Emojis
For informal digital methods, the use of emojis is one way to make sure that a less serious tone is imparted. By adding a smiley face to the end of a sentence that could be read in

a less than friendly way, you can make your intended tone much clearer.

Not everyone is a fan of using emojis, and they are sometimes best avoided when communicating with a person you don't know very well, or when the context is more formal. Depending on your company's policies and culture, they can sometimes be used in internal emails between colleagues to make the sound a little friendlier. It's always better to not go overboard with emojis, and if you're unsure if they're appropriate then don't use them.

When in doubt, ask another person for feedback before you send the message. If you can't do that, try reading the message aloud instead to see how it might sound in somebody else's mind.

Examples Of Tone In Written Communications

Here are a few examples of the same email message but written in different tones. Read through them and decide how the tone is likely to be interpreted by the majority of people:

A. *You haven't sent the completed report to me yet. It needs to be finished and approved by tomorrow. If you fail to send the report in time, we could lose the account. I expect to receive the report for approval before 5pm today.*

B. *The deadline for sending the report to the client is tomorrow. Please send the completed report to me before 5pm for approval so that we don't lose the account.*

C. *I need to send the report to the client tomorrow, so that we can retain the account. It'll take me a few hours to read through and approve it, so please can you send it across to me by 5pm today? Let me know if you need any further details.*

All three of these emails contain the same information, but the way the recipient interprets the tone will vary. Personal filters aside, the specific word choices in these emails are likely to provoke certain reactions on the reader.

The email A is quite sharp, and it uses language that could be considered as blaming language. It could be interpreted that the sender is frustrated, and that they wanted the report to be sent earlier. The repeated use of *'You'* in a negative manner reinforces the blaming tone. Most people reading this would be mildly offended, or concerned that they were in trouble with the sender.

Email B is likely to be read as less accusatory, but still slightly negative. It's also quite passive in terms of the voice used. It's unlikely to cause major offence, but it's still very cold and clinical.

The last email is more collaborative and has no blaming language. It reinforces the message that the account could be lost but does this in a more positive way, framing it as 'keeping the account' by sending the report in time. It is still clear in terms of what's expected but has a much more relaxed tone.

In most situations, the third email is the most appropriate. However, depending on the context and the sender's past experiences with the recipient it could be that a sharper tone is necessary.

Depending on the recipient's own filters, they might perceive the first two as too sharp, or they might simply see them as appropriately direct under the circumstances. None of these emails are *'right'* or *'wrong'*– they are simply examples of how the same message can be conveyed quite differently with a few changes in word choice.

The Benefits of Good Written Communication

Good written communication skills are a great skill to put on your resume. With more and more remote workers, and teams working across different offices, companies are reliant on messaging services and emails to keep communication open across teams. Being able to, not only relay information succinctly, but also display the right tone is a great skill to have in these situations.

There are lots of other reasons to brush up your written skills. Being able to clearly convey the full message, including tone, makes misinterpretation much less likely. While there's rarely an accurate recording available of a conversation you have face-to-face, almost everything you send in writing is recorded and stored somewhere. When there's a potential record of what was said, it's even more important to be able to say exactly what you mean.

Our relatively recent obsession with social media can cause some communication issues, especially when there's a large age gap between participants. It's generally accepted that social media is very informal, but for people who have grown up with social media, that playful and sometimes irreverent tone can creep into work or more formal emails. This can potentially offend older generations who read this as rudeness. Conversely, those people used to more formal communication could believe their written communication is in a light friendly tone, but could be taken as too stiff and serious for the context by others.

Just like verbal communication, having an assertive style works well in most written communications. If in doubt, stick to these principles.

The key principles translated for written communications are:

- Active listening: reading the other person's messages carefully and making sure you acknowledge their points calmly and clearly.
- Direct but non-confrontational: Using clear language, an active voice and avoiding the use of blaming language by using 'I' statements instead of 'you.'
- Demonstrating empathy and appreciation for other people's point of view.
- If you don't know something, don't pretend that you do: Ask for more time to find the answer and provide a timescale for when you will respond with the information they need.

The purpose of any communication is to have our message understood by the recipient. When a message needs to be conveyed to a lot of people at the same time, email is often the easiest way to do this. Unfortunately, if the message isn't written in the right tone, it can cause confusion, frustration and additional work.

The overall benefits of good written communication are similar to those for verbal communication. You'll be able to clearly and confidently put across your views and opinions in a way that others can understand. You'll gain more respect from others for your well-written communications and you'll build and maintain better relationships.

Real Life Case Study – David

David managed a department of 200 people and had been given the task of cutting costs. After some investigation, he decided that an effective way to do this would be to reduce the overtime being paid out. He'd identified that there were some unnecessary overtime shifts happening and wanted to reduce these. His intended solution was making sure that any overtime shifts longer than four hours were approved beforehand by a manger.

On a Thursday evening, he sat down to type the email that would go to the entire department. He wrote:

Where employees are required to work hours in excess of their regular duty assignment, and where that work is estimated to require four or more hours outside of regular working hours, a manager's approval must henceforth be sought before commencement of the aforementioned work. Such approval is required to be in writing, and must be dated no later than twenty-four hours before the commencement of any proposed additional work.

When he arrived at the office on Friday morning, he already had twenty emails asking him to clarify what he meant. By Friday afternoon, over half of his department had sent emails asking for clarity. Frustrated, he showed the email to the company's communications manager, who offered some advice on rewording the email.

Late that afternoon, he sent out an amended version which read:

Any overtime shifts of four hours or more must be approved by your manager. Please make sure that you have written approval at least twenty-four hours before your overtime shift begins.

This time, he only received two emails asking for further information.

Like any other skill, developing good written communication skills takes time and practice. However, by applying the learning in this chapter to your written communications, you should find that you are receiving more positive responses and reducing misunderstandings.

The Most Important Skill for a Happy Productive Life

Effective communication is an extremely important skill to have. In this book, we've looked at the reasons why communicating effectively is essential in all areas of life. Your work and your personal life both benefit enormously from good communication skills.

Remember that the first rule of effective communication is:

The success of the communication is the responsibility of the communicator.

By taking on board the information presented in this book, you are accepting the responsibility and making progress towards becoming a better communicator.

Let's take a quick look at what we've covered:

There are four basic common communication types: *Passive, Aggressive, Passive-Aggressive* and *Assertive*. Having a good understanding of these four basic styles of communication can help you understand how you are communicating, and how that might come across to others. It will also help you recognize when you may be able to change the way you communicate in order to connect better with the person you are speaking to.

The best kind of communication is **assertive**, and we've covered lots of tips and techniques to help you become a more assertive communicator. Implementing these should provide improvements in your relationships at work and home, as well as making you more confident in getting your message across clearly.

Active listening happens when you put distractions to one side and focus completely on the person speaking and what they are saying. By listening without adding your own viewpoint or applying judgment to what they are saying, you can understand and acknowledge the other person's viewpoints. This can help you gain trust and avoid potential conflicts.

Active listeners not only hear what's being said, but they also notice the way the message is communicated. They are great at reading between the lines of a conversation because they pick up on all the verbal and non-verbal cues. These cues help you to understand the whole message the speaker is really trying to get across.

Body language helps you read between the lines of what people are saying. Even when their words and their tone of voice are delivering one message, the signals they send via their body language can show a different message. By looking for and identifying these inconsistencies, you can gain a better understanding of how someone is feeling.

Body language also helps you identify how others are perceiving the message you are delivering to them. By identifying what their facial expressions and body language are communicating, you can adapt your communication to be more effective and better understood.

Eye contact is important if you want to appear genuine and sincere, but it's important not to overdo it. Holding eye contact for too long can make people feel uncomfortable.

Mindset is important in communication. We often unconsciously project our beliefs via our word choices and choosing to have a positive growth mindset can change the way we speak about ourselves.

Conflict is a necessary part of communicating with others, but it doesn't have to be stressful. By understanding the different conflict management styles, and applying the five core concerns, most conflicts can be prevented or resolved without damaging relationships.

Communication skills are important in all aspects of life. Work, relationships, parenting our children or even just making small talk, all require an element of good communication. By making the commitment to develop your communication skills and become an assertive communicator, you're also making a commitment to forging success in all areas of your life.